Your Rose Will Bloom Again

by

Geri Coulter

Your Rose Will Bloom Again

by

Geri Coulter

This book is dedicated to my husband, Clifton,

and to my children: Kelly, Dustin, Kamela, and Cody.

They are the joy of my life.

Book cover artwork by Dustin Lee Coulter

Thanks to Steve Prager for help editing my first book

Table of Contents

~Appendix~

Acknowledgments

It is impossible to mention every person, group, and organization that has inspired me to write this book. While this is a personal spiritual autobiography, I have so many to thank for the walk with the Lord that I enjoy today. First, I must acknowledge my close and longtime dear friend, Denise Capra. She encouraged me to write down my stories so others could have hope. As a true and loyal friend, she is one of the precious few who know all about me and yet continue to love me anyway.

Floyd Price was the minister at the little Baptist church in Paoli, Indiana, where I was born again in 1970. Oh, what a glorious day! He mentored us, helped us to become soul winners, and was a real example of God's unconditional love and we are in touch with him to this day. The people in that church who took us under their wings were vital to our early Christian growth and development. Ray and Rosemary Trinkle were our guardian angels. Our friends: Darrell and Mary Anne Wilson, Randall and Donna Jones (and many others as the years rolled by), were all influential in our growth in grace, and we are still very close in the Lord.

Bible teachers and ministers Andrew Wommack, Kenneth Hagin, Kenneth Copeland, Oral Roberts (in the early days), and more recently Joseph Prince, Joel Osteen, Robert Morris and T.D. Jakes have been a tremendous influences on my Christian growth. I could continue: Dave and Bonnie Duell, Marilyn

Hickey, Kathryn Kuhlman, Paul and Jan Crouch and many others have impacted me for the glory of God.

But, at the end of the day, I have to say that the Lord Jesus is the Captain of my ship. Over the years, He has made many course corrections and divine interventions, and has always provided encouragement and leadership when I had no one else to turn to.

My husband and my children have enabled me to be free to serve the Lord; not hindering me in any way. They have always been my biggest fans. It is them I really feel the most compelled to acknowledge. Without them, I wouldn't be where I am, nor could I continue to fulfill my God-given calling to preach the Gospel to every creature.

A Word from the Author

The book you hold in your hands is the culmination of many years of experience living life. My life is a weaving of tragedy and triumph, just like everyone. People are all basically alike, and the same things happen to all of us. How we approach the trials of our lives determines how we emerge from each situation. God revealed to me the secret of joy – keeping the joy of the Lord – regardless of any external circumstances.

My story is simply a story of God's faithfulness. He keeps His promises. People call me strong; I tell them I'm not. Jesus is strong in me, through me, and it is His strength I lean on, walk in, and depend upon every day of my life.

People tell me constantly (even Charlie LeBlanc, when they lost their son, Beau), *"We knew if the Coulters are making it, we can make it."* And that was before we had lost our eldest son, Kelly. At the time, I can remember thinking, "How can Charlie and Jill even get dressed in the mornings?"

I was about to discover where that strength comes from.

We lost two homes to fire, Clifton's two brothers (one in our home fire), and a son to a tragic accident, all within a six-year period. There was also a church split, a devastating betrayal, during this time. Yet, God spoke to us at every turn, every circumstance, and brought new life to all our situations. He will do the same for you!

My goal in writing my story is to give hope to the hopeless and to cause faith to rise in people who've come to the end in their minds. Life is hard. There are those suffering through hard times who give up right before their miracle. My prayer is that this book, my spiritual autobiography, will inspire hope – hope that comes by the Word of God and by the word of our testimony (see Revelation 12:11). If God has done great things for me, He will do them for anybody who will reach out and believe Him.

This isn't a teaching book, but rather a testimony of my personal walk with the Lord and how He has delivered me from some of the most devastating circumstances known to the human heart. He will deliver you as well. He desires to give you joy unspeakable. God wants us to enjoy this life until we are in the real life ahead of us, eternal life. Joy in this life is not only possible, it's a sure thing!

I pray that you will enjoy and receive help from this book. It has my heart poured into it.

Believe me, your rose will bloom again.

Chapter 1

Your Rose Will Bloom Again

I remember it like it was yesterday – the first time I heard the phrase, "*Your rose is gonna bloom again!*" It was 1975; two years before my husband Clifton and I answered the call upon our lives to preach the gospel full-time.

To be completely honest – which I am aiming to be in this book – we would've been considered backslidden or 'away from God' by our own church, or any religious group, at the time we answered that calling. We'd just moved back to Indiana from Florida, where we'd lived for three years. We were staying with Clifton's brother Ivan and his family, near Paoli, while we looked for a place to live. That Sunday morning, as I was getting ready for church, Clifton was watching TV. When I walked into the living room to hear Oral Roberts' preaching, Clifton told me he felt Brother Roberts was speaking directly to him! I began to listen and the message was, "Your Rose is Gonna Bloom Again."

To give you a little background on us: We had moved away from Paoli and our church in 1972 – all the way to Florida – because we were disillusioned with church. We'd only been saved for two years when we discovered people aren't God! We hadn't yet learned the lesson that church leaders are human and don't always make the right decisions (it was a tough lesson to learn, but necessary in order to move forward). To make matters worse, we discovered that the church leaders in Florida were the same way – flawed! So, we fell back into some of our old ways. After a while, I thought if we could just get back home to Indiana, we would be okay.

So, here was Brother Roberts telling his audience that God would give you a new start every day – that there is hope to begin again – and he was using Isaiah 35:1, *"The desert shall rejoice and blossom as the rose."* I had no idea at the time how that verse would impact, not only my life, but the lives of thousands of people all over the world.

When I began to write this book in 1986, it was simply a testimony of how God healed our marriage. I had remembered the 'rose blooming again' message, applied it to my marriage, and God had delivered us and healed us. As a result, that message became my theme in life!

After the marriage restoration, I thought I was home free, but I had no idea how I would need the "rose revelation" over and over and over again. Now, as I look back over my Christian life, I can testify that every desert place I've walked through has blossomed as the rose – sometimes in a small way – just for me, and sometimes in a tremendous way that everyone could see. God has always shown Himself to be the Savior He proclaims to be. My deliverer and my peace; my comfort and my Lord.

Our Road to Damascus Transformation

Clifton and I were born again in 1970 in a little Baptist church on South Gospel Street in Paoli, Indiana. It was a quaint, small church until Clifton Coulter got saved. Then it exploded! Clifton had a reputation for being a drinker, a fighter; a man who was definitely not church material. He had settled down some after we'd gotten married and had our first son, Kelly, because we both wanted something better for Kelly than how we had lived our lives.

We thought church would be a good thing, and had tried out a church or two around the time the Baptist men came to tell us about the saving power of Jesus. Because of their testimony, we were born again in June, 1970. Our lives changed dramatically! It was a "road to Damascus" transformation (Acts 9:3). Black to white – literally overnight.

Our language changed, our circle of friends changed, and we dedicated our lives to God; to serving Him. We became instant soul winners. Clifton went out four nights a week with our young preacher – fresh out of seminary – who'd come to pastor our little Baptist church. We were his first congregation.

Now, I understand that Clifton was worth more than his weight in gold to that preacher! I also got very involved and became the Outreach Leader for the ladies. I was on every committee there was: Flower and Social, Finance, Secretary, Bible School, and Prayer. I did the bulletins, led the ladies group, sang in the choir, and also ministered in a ladies musical trio.

The church grew so fast that first summer that we had to move to a bigger building. When Clifton first got saved, the preacher asked him, "Do you know any lost people?" Clifton's answer was, "You're the only person I know who is saved!" There were over 100 baptisms that first summer. People continued to be saved, and the devil got madder by the day.

Eventually, there was so much trouble in the church that Clifton and I just wanted to run away. So we did. Clifton's brother, Phillip, had offered him a job in Margate, Florida. By that time, we had another baby boy: Dustin Frederick, so we loaded up our stuff and our kids and moved a thousand miles away. As we were packing, the preacher came to our home and gave us a letter to read later, after he'd left. He told us he was also leaving the church.

His letter was wonderful. He told us how much we'd meant to him and his wife. I still remember the words he wrote to me: "Geri, your soul, like Mary's, doth magnify the Lord." Coming from him, that was an awesome compliment! I was taken aback by the things he wrote to us. I hadn't realized how valuable we were to him.

We moved to Margate, Florida and became active in the Baptist church there. Eventually, we headed up the bus ministry and directed the children's church. We had another man driving one of the buses and we picked up over 150 kids on Sundays and brought them to church. Clifton would draw with chalk (he is an artist) and tell a Bible story. I led singing and we had refreshments.

We did all this knowing basically nothing! God had us in boot camp, training us, and we had not a clue. We were just faithful. We went out on Saturdays and invited kids to church, then went back out and picked them up on Sunday mornings. I'm still amazed when I think of how we blundered around, not knowing anything except we desired to serve the living God. In that Florida church, I sang in a gospel trio with a girl who had sung backup for the Rambos. We sang Dottie Rambo's songs. What great joy!

Dreams and Holy Rollers

I had a dream while we lived in Florida. I can almost count on one hand the 'God' dreams I've had – only two have been spiritual dreams. This one was so amazing, yet I didn't realize the impact it would have on us. Back then, I knew nothing about spiritual dreams or warning-type dreams.

My dream was a scene where Clifton had his Bible open in his hand, preaching to a sea of people as far as we could see. Innumerable faces. It was in Florida.

Clifton also had a warning dream about that same time. His dream was that he was in a casket, and we were back in Paoli. He wasn't really dead, and he saw the people we'd been in church with in Indiana, walking by the casket, shaking their heads like, "If only he had done things differently."

Combined with my dream, we were pondering those things in our hearts!

Actually, Clifton was running from the call to preach. He had approached me in Indiana soon after we were saved and said he believed the Lord was calling him to preach. I said, "I will never be a preacher's wife, and don't ever say that to me again!" I was ignorant of God's love. I thought I had to be like the only preacher's wife I knew, and I couldn't be like her. She was sweet, but she didn't wear jeans or boots; hardly wore any makeup, never played cards or went swimming, and those were all things I loved to do! I knew I couldn't change that much.

You see, I had no idea back then that God wanted me just as I was. He loved me so much He just wanted me to be myself! Those "ways" of the pastor's wife were not Jesus' ideas, but religious rules she received from the way she was raised. I didn't know that at the time. I admired her exceedingly, and loved her.

Before we left Florida, we visited a Full Gospel church one Wednesday night. Some friends of ours from the Baptist church said they'd gone over to an Assembly of God church, and that someone had spoken in tongues, and they'd seen a person get healed! I was excited. I thought, "Woo Hoo! I think I want to find out about this!" We'd seen a program on TV where Kathryn Kuhlman was interviewing guests who had received miracles in her meetings, so I was interested, but didn't know what to do.

Unfortunately, that A/G (Assembly of God) church was dead the night we went. No messages in tongues, nobody got healed – nothing happened. We were disappointed, so back to the Baptist church we went.

The Call

Simultaneously, something was going on with Clifton. We didn't understand that he was running from the call to preach. After I said I would *never* be a preacher's wife, he didn't mention it again. However, Clifton began to have serious health problems: he couldn't breathe and would go from room to room, then outside, and could get no relief. Later, we found out they were anxiety (panic) attacks. That condition is from the pit of hell, but back then we knew nothing of the spiritual realm. We were just trying to survive. Clifton's 'not being able to breathe' episodes were getting closer together, so I called a lung specialist one day while Clifton was at work. The lady I spoke with told me, "Honey, you don't need a lung doctor. Let me give you a number to call."

So I called the number. I reached the office of a psychiatrist! When I described Clifton's symptoms, the nurse said, "There is something going on with him that he can't cope with, something he doesn't want to face." She told me the next time he had an attack to get out a brown paper bag and have him breathe in and out of it slowly to balance the carbon dioxide and level him out. We did that for several weeks and then it grew to months. In the meantime, Clifton began to smoke and drink again. We'd both quit when we got saved.

Now, we were going to dinners with people in the horse business that had lots of money. Clifton was doing some work for them, so they would take us out to eat at fancy places and order drinks. That's why we felt backslidden. (By the way, forty years later, I now know that a believer in Jesus Christ who is born again cannot be backslidden. It's not even a New Testament term.) But at the time, I would go into the restroom and pray, "Oh, Jesus, please don't come tonight while I'm in this place!" I believed I would split hell wide open if I wasn't right with God and the Rapture occurred!

I'm saddened today as I realize that this is still the mindset of thousands of believers all over the world. I eventually learned about the unconditional love of God – I learned that as His children, He never lets go of us! Even when we try to let go of Him, we can't. The Father taught me grace through the love I have for my own children: no matter what they do, I still love them and would never cut them off.

Clifton's Background

Let me interject some of Clifton's background here. He was the youngest of five children; the baby. The Coulter name was well respected due to his dad's hard working lifestyle and honest, forthright reputation. His dad, Clifford, had no brothers or sisters, so Clifton's cousins weren't his first cousins, although he has always been close to them. The three Coulter Brothers: Phillip, Ivan, and Clifton, may have taken more after their grandfather, Thomas Reister, who also had a reputation. He was a tough sheriff and a tavern owner.

Grandpa Reister also drank a lot and so did the Coulter boys. Their alcohol addiction caused deep pain to their families, and also prevented the potential release of their many gifts – especially their incredible talent to break, train and raise horses. The Coulters had owned the "Triple C Quarter Horse

Farm" in Hardinsburg, Indiana. The downfall of the business was alcohol.

Clifton was popular in school. We both attended and graduated from Paoli High School. Clifton graduated in the class of 1962. I'm from the 1966 class. Clifton's first six years of school were in a one-room country schoolhouse! Phonics were removed from the schools either the year Clifton was born, or the year he started first grade (1950), and I, for real, thought the devil had a plan to keep him from learning to read even then! (The Word of God, when read or heard, is life and power. Thankfully, God did supernaturally teach Clifton to read when he answered the call to ministry in 1977.)

We didn't get together until years after we were out of school. Clifton was always a charismatic personality. He played sports and performed in the class plays. His mother told me he didn't have to act – he was that person! Ha. It was the Wilbur plays. Wilbur was a carefree, non-committal teenage boy, lying around on the couch and being very funny! Everyone liked him.

I fell in love with Clifton from a distance – just watching him – from the time I was in junior high school. He never knew, of course, because he dated the cheerleaders and basketball queens! I looked up to whoever Clifton decided to date. There was one girl he loved, who he gave a diamond ring to after his senior year. He'd dated her for seven years. Her M.O. was: she'd break up with him until Clifton found a new girlfriend, then she wanted him back. It was the same story when Clifton and I were planning to be married. She showed up at a friend's home, where Clifton had been invited for supper, after work. She asked him if he was really going to marry "that little Grimes girl." Clifton let her know he was serious! So after that, she got married to another fella, then divorced, but she never caused us any more problems.

I Married an Alcoholic

I didn't know I was marrying an alcoholic. Clifton worked hard and was a weekend or after-work alcoholic. He would never stop drinking as long as there was anything to drink, unless he passed out first. Those days were difficult; very hard on me as a young bride.

From our first date together, we didn't go back and forth, dating other people or breaking up, etc. Our first date was in February, and we were married in June of 1968. We spent two years loving each other, but having significant issues with Clifton's drinking. Jesus saved us 'just in time.' That story is ahead!

Chapter 2

A Breakthrough from Heaven in '77

Clifton and I decided we should move back to Indiana. The company he worked for offered him a lucrative job as superintendent of their construction company, headquartered in Michigan. We knew that job would mean Clifton would have to work away from home, which neither of us liked, but we wanted to get out of Florida. His company paid for our move, so we packed up our stuff and our (now) three kids – Kamela Joy was born in Florida – and we all headed back home.

Financially, we were good, but spiritually, we were bankrupt, even though we could see God's hand in our lives. We'd prayed for a baby girl. We had the two adventurous boys, full of life and little boy stuff. They were such a joy, but we wanted a little girl, and I can still remember the happiness we experienced when Kami Joy was born.

A Big Lesson to Learn

Our friends in Indiana were ecstatic that we were back, and we picked up right where we left off. We went back to church, and as far as they knew, we were just like we were when we'd left. But we weren't. We thought God was mad at us, and we felt we had a lot of making up to do! And yet, Oral Roberts' message: our rose blooming again – a message about new beginnings – was still giving us hope.

After we'd been back home for about a year – by that time we'd been born again for seven years – something happened at church that rocked our world. We hadn't yet learned the lesson that church leaders are fallible. Looking to God and Jesus Christ is the only way to joy and peace. Putting trust in any man is a huge mistake.

What happened was this: that Sunday, the church leadership handled a situation with a fellow church member in a way that neither Clifton nor I could stomach. The man – whom we loved – had been treated in a very un-Christian manner at the front door of the church. Our friend had been asked to leave and never come back! He was thrown right out of the church! So now what?

On Monday morning, Clifton went back to work, and I was at home, pondering everything. I was confused and discouraged. There'd been a reason for pause and consideration due to the accusations leveled against our church friend, but my thoughts were, "Is this a Jesus-like decision?" I was so preoccupied with the whole situation that I caught myself putting the salt and pepper in the refrigerator and other bizarre acts! I didn't call anyone on the phone; I didn't talk about it with anyone. I just prayed and cried. I stayed at home and took care of my children.

That was the fall of 1976. Clifton used the whole mess as an excuse to skip church, and he began, I discovered later, to drink heavily while he was away at work. I continued to go to church and do my duties, but I was just going through the motions.

A Miracle in the Mail

Then one very important day, I received a book in the mail, sent to me by Sandy Coulter, my sister-in-law in Florida. She'd had it sent to me from Tulsa. It was called "A Daily Guide to Miracles" by Oral Roberts. I don't remember what I thought, but I laid it on the table and didn't look at it right away, even though I remembered Oral had preached the message on "Your Rose is Gonna Bloom Again," which had impacted my husband and I in such a powerful way. Then, in December 1976, I was working in the kitchen of our rented home in Valeene, Indiana, when I heard an enthusiastic voice come over the TV.

"You're gonna get a breakthrough from Heaven in '77," the TV voice said. I ran to see who it was, because my insides had leapt for joy and I didn't even know what my spirit was. (Later, I learned that my spirit, joined to the Holy Spirit, had grabbed that word with great force.) The voice belonged to Brother Oral, and I stood and listened with my whole heart to everything he said. I knew my breakthrough was on the way! I was so ignorant of spiritual things that I had no idea what a breakthrough was, but I knew it was something wonderful, and I was going to get one!

I immediately began to read Brother Roberts' book that I'd left lying on the table. Isn't God the most awesome Person? Isn't

He smart? It's just overwhelming to me to realize how He loves us and how He has a plan for each one of us.

Our part is so easy. Just listen and obey. I didn't know what I was doing, but my love for God and the gratitude I felt for my salvation was deeper and wider than my offense towards the people at church. Even though they'd made questionable decisions, I still knew God was good and that He loved all of us. (Folks make a big mistake by quitting God after they realize their church isn't perfect.)

Bad Devil, Good God

I remember in the very first chapter, Brother Roberts was talking about the devil, and how he's the one who causes bad things to happen to us. I'd never heard such a thing! I'd always thought, "Everything happens for a reason," "God is in charge," and "Everything that happens in our lives is from Him."

The truths in Oral's book transformed my life! My eyes were opened. (It is always the truth of the Word of God that opens us to the revelation we need from the Spirit of God.)

Here's what I learned: God is good – always and in every way. He never wants bad things to happen to us, but we live in a sinful world. *All creation groans to have Him revealed* (Romans 8:22). Even creation suffers from the sin that is here because of Adam's disobedience. In the book of James, we read, "*Let no man say when he is tempted that he is tempted of God, for God tempts no man.*" (James 1:17, emphasis mine)

The word "tempt" in that verse also means "test." God tests no man. Jesus stood the test for us.

I buried myself in the Word of God. "The Daily Guide to Miracles" got me into my Bible and I was reading things I'd never heard from any of my pastors. I had to see if it was really true. And WOW is all I can say! During that time an old friend, Marge, whom I hadn't heard from in a long time, called me. We had led her husband to the Lord, and then they went beyond where we were spiritually, and received the baptism in the Holy Ghost. It all happened while we were in Florida. I remembered hearing that they'd felt that they had to leave the Baptist church.

One day, while we still lived in Florida, she called me at home. Clifton was never home during the day, but that day he'd left something at the house and had to return to pick it up, and so he was at home when the call came. Marge said she had a prophetic word for my husband. She said the Lord had spoken to her to give Clifton the word, and she called, after saying to the Lord, "If he answers, I'll know to speak to him." Clifton did answer! That was something we didn't understand, and I don't remember what the word was, exactly, except that it was an encouraging, good word. We were impressed and blessed!

So, here she was, calling again, asking me what was going on, how we were, etc. I told her I'd received Oral's book, and she excitedly said, "Read Chapter 10 and call me back!" It was the chapter on the baptism in the Holy Spirit!

I must interject something here. My two best friends in the world, Donna and Mary Anne, felt the same way I did about what had happened at the church. We were some of the hardest workers in the church. We were all disillusioned and hurt. I hadn't spoken with Donna or Mary Anne in a while. We were all sitting at home licking our wounds, trying to figure out what had happened at the church regarding our friend.

At the same time, I was getting more and more interested in going deeper with the Lord. It seemed to me that the Holy Spirit baptism was the way to go. I had a desire to share this with my friends, Mary Anne and Donna, so I invited them down to my house. This was early 1977, maybe March. Amazingly, they were on the same page. What a thrill it was to share with them, and we were all just wild about the possibility that there was more than what we'd experienced with God so far. Donna even said she'd been having dreams that she was speaking in tongues and I said, "Oral Roberts did the same thing!" (My husband laughs about that to this day!) It just goes to show you, God is no respecter of persons. Oral Roberts was a legend, and Donna was a little mom and housewife, seemingly insignificant to the world, and yet God showed them both the same thing!

Mary Anne shared an experience she'd had when my friend Marge prayed for her. Mary Anne explained feeling a warm sensation in her body (even in her teeth), and that Marge prayed a prayer for Mary Anne that included things Marge couldn't possibly have known about in the natural realm. We didn't know about the gifts of the Holy Spirit back then; we just pondered those things in our hearts. We were so excited that God had been dealing with all of us in the same way.

I Receive the Power

So, I called Marge back (after I read chapter 10), and she prayed with me on the phone. Later, I got down on my knees in my living room, after I had put the children to bed, and I asked God to fill me with the Holy Ghost. *Ask and you shall receive!* (Matthew 7:7)

First of all, I was instantly delivered from nicotine. Then, I felt something I'd never experienced before. It was like a flood of pure love pouring over me – a love that I never knew existed. I don't know how long I stayed on the floor, but I got up from there a different person. My breakthrough from Heaven had begun!

That was in April, 1977. I called Marge and told her what had happened to me. She was so excited. She and her husband Rodney had started a fellowship in Salem, a close-by town, and they invited our singing group to come minister at their church. The group was: me, Donna, Mary Anne, and another lady, Penny, who'd been singing with us since 1970. "How awesome," we thought, so we trooped over there; husbands in tow. Our men folk were skeptical, but we all loved each other so much, and we were so interested in what the Salem people had discovered about the spiritual side of life. Also, our men wanted to know what in the world had happened to their wives!

As we began to sing that evening, something changed. Back then, we had no clue what the anointing was, but that was what came over us. It was the best we'd ever sounded! Our harmonies came through like angels. We hardly recognized ourselves. It also seemed that there were other voices (angels?)

coming from the platform where we stood. (We talked about it later for hours – it was amazing.) Also, the church people were lifting their hands high during our singing, and we were taken so off-guard that we didn't know what to do! I remember the whole thing sort of scared me.

At the end of the service, Rodney, the preacher, asked if anyone needed prayer, and I went forward. I told him I was afraid. He spoke to my mind and my body to let go of any fear, and I actually FELT something leave my body. I was standing by a window, and I remember thinking, "It went out that window." My friend Mary Anne received prayer and then fell on the floor! I'd held onto Rodney's arm, because I felt like I was going to fall, and I wondered, "What is this?" It was a very peaceful, wonderful sense of warm oil flowing over me. But Mary Anne – I was bewildered! I saw her smiling and I knew she was okay, but the whole thing was way outside my realm of understanding.

Later, I searched my Bible to locate anything I could use to explain what had happened. I found all the scriptures I needed. I also read "They Speak with Other Tongues" by John Sherrill. He had set out to disprove those things and ended up filled with the Holy Ghost himself and became a believer. Isn't that just like God?

We were invited back, week after week, to sing at their church, and we loved it! Penny did drop out of our little group, but today (in 2015) she knows all about it, because she went to Heaven early.

A Holy Ghost Trap is Set

Marge called me one day. It was April 1977, and we talked about Clifton. I told her I knew he had a call on his life, but that he was further away from preaching than he'd ever been. She said, "Let's fast and pray!" I had no idea about fasting – all I knew was it meant not to eat – so we fasted with liquids only, and prayed. We did it for a few days. I think maybe three.

We set up a meeting at Mary Anne's and her husband Darrell's house for that coming Friday night. Normally, every weekend, Clifton and I and our friends would get together and play cards or Monopoly. I told Clifton we were invited to Mary Anne's to eat supper and play cards that Friday night. Clifton knew Darrell had been going with us to the meetings in Salem, and he really didn't want to go to their house. I'd become a crazy woman, in his opinion, with all my Bible reading and those other books I had gotten ahold of. I was constantly trying to tell him how wonderful it was to know the power of God! Well, he finally agreed to go to the card party.

In reality, Mary Anne and I had set up a 'Holy Ghost' meeting, and invited Rodney and Marge (the Pentecostal preachers) and some friends from the Baptist church who we thought wanted more of God. It was gonna be a Holy Ghost meeting – or meetin', if you know what I mean!

Chapter 3

Clifton's Second "Road to Damascus" Experience

The morning we were to go eat supper and play cards, I was feeling guilty about deceiving my husband into going up there, knowing that the Pentecostal preachers were going to be there too. I said, "Honey, there is something I need to tell you about tonight." Clifton immediately said he didn't want to hear anything about it. He said, "I said I'd go and I will, but I don't want to hear another word about it!"

"Oh, hallelujah!" I thought. I was rejoicing. Jesus had let me off the hook! (Jesus will always get you off the hook.)

Friday night came.

The first part went well. We had meat, biscuits, gravy and other good stuff. Mary Anne is a great cook. After supper, the others began to arrive. Clifton looked at me like he wanted to get his hands around my throat when he saw the preachers coming up the sidewalk. He was NOT happy! There were several other couples there. We talked, we laughed, and then Marge and Rodney asked if we could have prayer.

We were all in a circle in the living room, sitting in chairs. They went around the room praying, exercising the gifts of the Spirit in healings, words of knowledge; different things. Then, they came to Larry, one of Clifton's work buddies. As Clifton describes it, it took all Clifton had, spiritually, to keep Larry straight all week while they were away at work.

After Larry was prayed for, he fell out onto the floor and had the look of an angel on his face. He began to roll down the floor! (Our first experience with a real, live HOLY ROLLER!) Clifton's thoughts were, "When they lay hands on me, I will roll on the ceiling," because of course, he was more spiritual than Larry! Smile.

The Best Night of Our Lives

Then, they laid their hands on Clifton and prayed with all their hearts. Nothing happened. Nothing. After the circle of prayer was concluded, people started to leave. Larry's wife led him out. He was drunk in the Spirit, we learned later, but at the time we didn't know what in the world had happened to him. Donna's husband, Randall, was in the kitchen after the prayer circle broke up, and he told Clifton he'd opened his eyes during the prayer, and saw the feet of Jesus standing in the middle of the room. He said he didn't look any further, but instead, shut his eyes back tight! We knew it was true. Clifton asked him, "What do you think of this?" Randall said, "I don't know, but I know it's God." (Randall knows all the truth now, as he went to be with the Lord a few years later.)

Clifton went into a room near the back of the house and stayed in there for a very long time. While he was in the room praying, Marge was praying for the women in another room, and we were experiencing being "slain in the spirit." (Being slain in the spirit is a phenomenon that happens when humans are overcome by God's anointing and presence, and are unable to stand.) Some ladies were receiving the prayer language of the Holy Spirit – speaking in tongues. It was a fabulous night!

One lady in the prayer circle received a healing for her knee, and she was interested in finding out more. We all were. It was the most outstanding and outrageous night of our lives, and we have gone back to the memory of that night many times in order to keep on track and to be able to stay in the ministry. Little did we know – the best was yet to come.

When Clifton came out of the back room, Larry was being led out of the house, still grinning from ear to ear; the Spirit of God all over him. His wife had to drive home. Clifton asked Rodney, "What's wrong with me, why didn't I get anything?" Rodney laughed and said, "I don't know, what does God want you to do?"

According to Clifton, hearing that question was like being hit with a sledge hammer! Clifton knew exactly what God wanted him to do. Larry (the Holy Roller) was one of the last to leave, and soon the only ones left there were us, our hosts Mary Anne and Darrell, and the preachers. By this time, it was past midnight. We gathered up our kids, Clifton put his cap on (advertising Pete's Hog Feed), and we started to leave. In his black T-shirt pocket was a cigarette pack with two Camel cigarettes in it. On our way to the door, Clifton pulled the cigarettes out of his pocket and asked Rodney, "Do you think

God could take these away from me?" Both Rodney and Marge said, "Sure! Just sit down here." They pointed to a chair in the middle of the living room, which was thereafter named the "hot seat." Smile.

Clifton's testimony is that when he sat down, he was saying, "Yes," to God – whatever that meant. The preachers prayed for him. To get the full effect, you really need to hear Clifton tell his story in person, in his own words. We do have a set of testimony CDs, updated and revised. For now, I will do my best to tell the story – which could have a place in the book of Acts!

Clifton's Acts 29 Experience with God

First, as they were praying, they asked him to lift his hands. Clifton said he couldn't. Everyone thought it was because he was a Baptist, but Clifton literally could not physically move. It was obvious he was experiencing something very different than he ever had before. Rodney said, "Shove him onto the floor." Clifton fell out of the chair and onto the floor with a little help. He was on his back, and they continued to pray for him. They had cast out the spirit of nicotine while he was still sitting in the chair, and asked him to blow out the spirit of addiction. Clifton obeyed, and he said it tasted like a cup of pure liquid nicotine was in his mouth. He blew it out, like they said, and the cigarette craving was gone for good!

While Clifton lay on the floor, the prayer continued, and the spirit of addiction to alcohol was cast out. Once and for all. He was healed of back problems: Clifton had been told by a doctor that he would be in a wheelchair by the time he was 40 years old (he was 33 at the time). Clifton's ulcers were also healed.

Then, Clifton lifted his hands and for nearly three hours he kept his arms and hands in the air, seeing visions and receiving revelation from God. He said his whole body tingled and felt like electricity was running through it. He spoke in tongues – he laughed, he cried – as did we all! At one point, I remember thinking, "He is going to die." My thought was that no one could be that close to God and live. I kept looking at Rodney, who by now was sitting in a chair, laughing. I thought, "How can he laugh? This is serious." Wow!

I'm Gonna P-P-P-P-Preach

I called Donna and Randall and held the phone out to this "Pentecostal" experience for them to hear. Daylight came. We ate donuts and cinnamon rolls and talked about what had happened to Clifton. He had accepted the call of God upon his life to preach the Gospel. God showed him the Bible, rolling across the ceiling like a negative – white letters on a black ceiling. Someone was circling little words with a white pen and the voice of the Spirit of God spoke to Clifton and said, "I am calling you to preach the little things others are missing." The meeting finally broke up around 8 a.m. that Saturday morning. This was around April 22, 1977.

On our way home – before we even got out of Darrell's driveway – we met a couple from our church who were filled with the Holy Ghost and had been praying for years for a Spirit-filled church to open in our town. I said, "Clifton, tell them what happened to you." Clifton said, "I'm gonna p-p-ppr-r-reach the Gospel!" He could hardly get it out, but when he did there was rejoicing in the driveway that morning! They became one of the four couples who would start the Lighthouse with us.

Chapter 4

The Lighthouse

Along with Darrell and Mary Anne Wilson, Terry and Linda Campbell (the couple we met in the driveway that morning), Randall and Donna Jones, and Rodney and Marge Chastain, we started the Lighthouse on August 7, 1977. There were 28 of us there, the first Sunday morning we met as a church. At the time, I knew nothing of Biblical numerology, but God did! August is the eighth month. NEW BEGINNINGS! Three sevens – seven is God's number of perfection and completion.

Between April and August we had home prayer meetings. We sang worship songs, prayed; we loved each other and were experiencing the power of the living God! We continued to go to the Baptist church, and had no intention of starting a church. It was unheard of in our area in the 70's.

Am I Invisible?

We actually thought everyone at the Baptist church would be ecstatic to hear about our newfound excitement, and would want to have the same experience we'd had. We were young and full of dreams, with a burning hot desire to serve the Lord.

We loved everyone at the Baptist church and we still do. However, at that time, they didn't understand us, even though we tried to explain.

Soon, we began to be left out of church things that we used to be in the middle of. We weren't even asked to pray anymore. I asked Clifton one Sunday morning, "Am I invisible?" I felt invisible. One morning, we pulled up in front of the church and couldn't go in, so we drove over to Salem where Rodney and Marge had their fellowship. They didn't call it a church.

Clifton and I have always been soul winners and we were constantly inviting people to come to church. The drawback to going to the Salem fellowship was that people from our area didn't want to make the 22 mile drive over there, so through a series of circumstances, we established our first church. Terry and Linda Campbell had been praying for many years for a Spirit-filled church to be started in our area. We had joined with the little group in Salem (who didn't call themselves a church), and we had never even heard of anyone starting their own church. We didn't know it was possible!

A few couples who were at the Friday night, "Acts Chapter 29" meeting at Mary Anne and Darrell's house (where Clifton had his Holy Spirit encounter), were interested in starting their own church. For one thing, we weren't welcome at the Baptist church anymore. (Now, as I look back, I understand – no hard feelings on our part.) Several members of that church had come to us privately and told us they loved us, and wished us well. They hoped we could have a successful church. Many of those same folks came to our churches, off and on, over the years.

As we met over the summer for Bible study, prayer and worship, the group grew too large to keep meeting in homes, so we started looking for a building.

Our First Church

We named our first church the Lighthouse. God provided everything we needed. Several Sunday school teachers – we had a large number of kids; a Treasurer (Terry), an Associate Pastor and Song Leader (Rodney) and even a piano player! There are no words to describe our elation. God provided a little country church building, it was 109 years old at the time, and hadn't been used in many years. We fixed it up, much like the one in the movie, "The Apostle." We cleaned, put on some new paint and flooring, and continued to improve the old building as we were able. It was provided for free!

At the time, Clifton had a good-paying job as a construction superintendent. We were building a house on fourteen acres of woods. It was our dream house. I'd picked out the plans, and Clifton was building it for me with his own two hands. He had helped others in the Baptist church build their homes, but by the time we began building ours, everyone was mad at us for our conversion to Holy Ghost beliefs, so we were on our own.

We take the blame for not handling ourselves with more wisdom concerning our Baptist church friends, but our zeal was unquenchable. It was out of control. All we wanted to do was tell people about what had happened to us, and that God would fill them with the Holy Spirit and heal them too – whatever they needed. He is the God of the impossible! This is what we were telling people, and we were doing it full time, except for sleep.

Soon, Clifton didn't have time to work, so we agreed he should quit his job. That was probably a big mistake. However, we did learn to trust God fully for everything. We didn't receive a salary from the church. Occasionally, the treasurer would give us a few dollars, but we were in a financial struggle which would last for a very long time.

Our church grew fast. We were seeing miracles every service and the townspeople were coming out to "that church" to see what was happening. We shot up to over 300 people in a very short period of time. Clifton dug a basement, and we added on to try to accommodate the people, but there still wasn't enough room. After seven years of ministry, we bought and moved to the Oak Grove Road facilities, twelve miles from Paoli, on the east side of town. We had been four miles south.

Our people wanted a Christian school for our kids and so we had that for twelve years. There were 65 students attending at one time. To house the school at the beginning, we bought a building in Marengo, a small town south of our church.

While we were in the first church building, we saw thousands of miracles. At the time, we thought that was normal for a Spirit-filled church and had no idea how phenomenal it really was! Looking back, if only we'd had some direction – someone to help us – things would have been different. Because, eventually, the spirit of anti-Christ had enough of us and our church, and he began a campaign: a campaign to destroy us, our church, and everyone in it.

The Miracles

Let me tell you a few of the most outstanding miracles that happened in our first church. A broken leg was healed between services one Sunday. Clifton had prayed for the woman that morning, and by Sunday night, she was healed and came to church showing us all. Another time, termites literally disappeared when Clifton rebuked them, and that same day a little boy's head was healed from a large goose egg bump he got during the service. A seven-year-old girl was healed of a rheumatic heart.

Our son, Kelly, who was eight years old at the time, saw Jesus appear in the church and place His hand on Clifton's head while he was preaching. Other miracles took place that same night: a small boy saw a white dove descend on the altar as people were being prayed for. Teeth were filled; people no longer needed glasses or hearing aids, and on and on I could go. Once, during a tent meeting in Crane Village, Indiana, Clifton prayed for a girl who was mentally handicapped. She improved and eventually was placed in regular classes, where she went to the top of her class and graduated high school with honors. Then, she graduated college!

One time, we sat at the bedside of a girl who had taken an overdose of pills and drunk a whole bottle of vodka. The hospital had given her family no hope, and they were making funeral arrangements when Clifton showed up. She was totally and completely healed by the next day (her sister had called us, after she'd attended our church and received the miracle of a filled tooth).

A teenager in our church took 100 Tylenol and destroyed her liver. She was on the liver transplant list, but the doctor told her mother that the girl would get progressively worse for five days and then die. Clifton went to the hospital and stayed, praying, until the girl was out of danger. She was totally and completely healed with no aftereffects, and today is a successful business woman, wife and mother. She attends our meetings whenever we go to Indiana.

Demon Encounters

Our first encounter with a demon is a powerful story! We had only been filled with the Holy Ghost for a short time, and our church was only about six months old. An old classmate from grade school and high school days came up to me at a Full Gospel Business Men's (FGBM) Fellowship meeting in Bedford, Indiana, a town about twenty miles north of Paoli. (The Full Gospel Business Men's meetings were one of the only places we had to go for teaching and training. I also attended and eventually started a Women's Aglow chapter. Clifton took some correspondence courses with the Assemblies of God.)

My old friend was there with her husband at the FGBM meeting. She said to me, "Would you come to our home and help us receive the Holy Spirit?" That was like saying, "Sic'um to a bulldog." as Clifton would say! Would we? Absolutely! So, we planned to go to their house for supper the following Friday night. She invited the whole family, which at that time was Kelly (8), Dustin (5), and Kami (3). This couple had four children about the same ages.

As soon as we arrived, I went to the kitchen to help my friend with the meal. Clifton was in the living room with her husband, and the kids went off to play in their big old fashioned house. I will call this man, the husband, Ben. Ben had many different translations of the Bible laying everywhere and stacks of teaching material. He was interested in God and in what we could tell him. It seemed like a piece of cake to minister to them. In the kitchen, his wife (I will call her Lois) was telling me things that were disturbing, but I was brand new and hadn't had any experience with demons. She said he'd been talking in his sleep and that there would be different voices coming from him – scary voices – and they were arguing about him killing himself. She said one voice was evil and deep and she was frightened. I thought, "Oh no!" and told her that it was probably just a dream.

We set the chili bowls on the table and all the drinks. It was a long table with at least twelve chairs. Lois had come from a big family, and I remember as a kid going to her house to eat. There were eleven of us that night. After we ate and the children had gone back to play, we began to share with them about the Holy Spirit. We said He was ready and willing to come into them.

One thing I had learned from a mentor, in the early days, was to always make sure the individual was saved before asking the Holy Spirit to come in. I asked, "Can we pray?" and the four of us joined hands. Clifton was praying the prayer, and asked him to say, "Jesus is Lord." Ben said he couldn't say it. Then, I began to pray, and I said, "Oh, Lord, just pour your love upon Ben, so that he will know your Presence."

As soon as I said that, Ben pulled his hands away and grabbed the sides of the table. Ben was a medium sized man with small arms, but he lifted up the table, from the end, while he was still seated! I mean a table covered with eleven chili bowls, glasses, and other dishes! He shook it violently, and all four table legs were off the ground like the table was levitating. It was something humanly impossible to do!

Then Ben began to speak in a different voice. The first thing he said was, "My face is dark and my eyes are black." Clifton and I looked at each other and thought, "What do we have here?" He continued to say, "I feel like I want to beat my face on this table." Clifton was thinking, "I'll help you."

"I'm Gonna Kill Somebody!"

Then the voice said, "I think I am going to kill somebody!" My mind was racing – I saw newspaper headlines, "Man Goes Berserk – Kills Minister and Family". Lois said, "I heard if you sing about the Blood, the demons have to flee." So, we sang every Blood song we knew! In the meantime, while we were singing, the Lord told Clifton to place his hands on the man's shoulders from the back and to not remove them. God also said, "Don't turn your back on him."

There was a conversation going on between the demon and Clifton, an argument about how powerful the demon was, and how that he was going to win. Clifton told him the devil was a loser and that Jesus had already won. During this time, Ben's facial features changed radically. I know it sounds bizarre, and we don't rehearse it too often, but his eyes turned a reddish color, his nose changed and he became the ugliest creature I'd ever laid my eyes on. Ben said he was going to win.

I had heard Rodney and Marge talk about casting out devils, so I decided I needed to call Rod. I called his phone (home line, no cells then) over and over and over. God wanted us to figure this one out on our own though, because I found out the next day that Rodney had been sitting in a chair beside his phone all that evening and it never rang.

Ben said things like he was the 'power,' and making himself out to be in control. He kept saying he was 'the winner.' Clifton began to use the name of Jesus and demanded the demon to come out of Ben. The commanding continued for a period of time, and then we witnessed something so supernatural that we were just simply amazed.

There were several demons. Suicide was one, Liar was another's name. The facial changes, the voice, it was all so terrible. Finally, Ben collapsed onto the table. He lay there for a few minutes, but it seemed like hours. When he came to, he looked normal again. Ben said at first he didn't remember what had happened. Then he said, "No, I do remember, I can't lie." Jesus won – Ben accepted Jesus as his Savior and was filled with the Holy Ghost!

Ben also said someone at the laundry mat had given him a book about idol worship. He went and got it, showed it to us, and said something happened to him when he read the book. Clifton took the book outside, struck a match to it as it lay on top of the deep snow, and the book disintegrated – burned all up – until there was nothing left but ashes. It was something else I'd never seen happen before! A book lying on top of snow does not burn like that.

Power In The Name

When we left that night we were beyond bewildered, but we were also much wiser in spiritual things! After we got home, I left the lights on for two solid weeks and I didn't sleep well for at least part of those two weeks. We were overwhelmed at the power of our God and the name of Jesus! There is POWER in the Name of Jesus.

I began to read books by all the deliverance preachers and authors, only to discover we'd done nothing right according to their instructions on 'how-to' cast out devils. They said, "Don't touch the person," and yet Clifton had kept his hands on Ben the entire two hours. There were also instructions on how to keep the demons from entering other people in the room, which we hadn't even known was a possibility. We just followed the Lord and got the desired results!

Ben, Lois and all the kids came to our church for years. Ben took some Bible school courses by correspondence, and I heard later that he became a minister. They moved away. Discovering that the Word was real and that we could depend on it transformed our lives and those we touched.

A New Beginning

After seven years in the country church building, we moved to the other side of town, twelve miles out in the middle of cow pastures and cornfields. We purchased a large house with a 6,000 square foot building (a former factory), on 14 acres, and we turned it into a beautiful church and Christian school. At the same time, however, we were in the fight of our lives with a spirit that was <u>not</u> God. The devil was trying hard to stop us in our tracks.

We were starting our eighth year of ministry at the new location. It was a new place for us. That is when God taught me about the number eight meaning new beginnings and the phrase "Your Rose Will Bloom Again" was reintroduced to me. Here's what I learned: God made the earth in six days. On the seventh day, He rested and on the eighth day there was a new beginning – a new week. There are seven steps leading from the outer court into the inner court. The eighth step leads to the Holy of Holies, the very presence of God. A new beginning for mankind! There were eight people on the ark – a new beginning for the world. That's when God spoke to me about a new beginning at our new place, Lighthouse II.

Chapter 5

Lighthouse II and New Beginnings

For seven years, we had given our all to God through the church work. We'd developed a TV and radio ministry, we'd traveled some, and worked hard at the school. By that time, the school taught daycare through the twelfth grade. I administrated the school, recorded daily radio broadcasts, taught in the school, kept the teachers and parents happy, helped as the co-pastor, traveled with our singing group and Clifton (when he preached outside the church) and took care of three children and our home. Whew!

It's difficult to explain this, but somehow I got the idea that if I gave 100% to God, He would take care of my family. As a result, the enemy used our love for God and the church and ministry to drive a wedge between Clifton and me. Our time was all used up for the church and the people in the church. Isn't it amazing how clever the enemy is? We always say the devil is dumb, but he knows what to do to get at us. My heart was towards God and His will, and all I wanted to do was fulfill what He'd called me to do. I know Clifton wanted that too, but he was deceived into thinking some things that were not true.

Marriage Troubles

I saw that we were in deep trouble concerning our marriage, and I didn't know what to do. I had no one to talk to.

Before we had entered the ministry, even though we had problems like everyone else, we had it made in the shade. Our three kids were amazing. They were beautiful, smart and perfectly healthy. Clifton made plenty of money. We had bought land and built a five bedroom, two-story house. As I mentioned earlier, it was my dream home. Clifton used to tell me he didn't think anyone in the world loved each other as much as we did. I agreed. We were crazy about each other.

When we answered the call to ministry and started our church, we thought everything was perfect. How could anything be any better than this? Following our call from God! However, the enemy of our souls – the spirit of anti-Christ – is a deceiver and the author of confusion and he set out to destroy us. I loved my husband intensely, but our lives got caught up in "doing the ministry," and it seemed like we had no time for each other.

So, we grew apart. It was a polarized time in our marriage and ministry. The church stuff was so exciting, but sadness descended when we went home and closed the doors! (There were a few brief intervals of fun and 'normal life.' We bought a Honda Goldwing motorcycle and traveled all over the country – something we both enjoyed.)

So while the church continued to grow past the 300 mark, our marriage relationship was disintegrating before my very eyes, and I was helpless to fix it. I did try. I prayed. I did all I knew to do. Clifton was deceived into thinking that I was only staying with him because I wanted to save the church. He thought all I cared about was the ministry and how it could go forward. That two-sided coin went on for over five years. By that time, we had celebrated our seven year church anniversary and we were going into our eighth year of ministry at the new facility (this was in 1984).

D-I-V-O-R-C-E?

God spoke to me that I was going to get a new beginning for the church and for our marriage during our eighth year, although it had been the worst year of my life until then. Clifton was distant, and one day he just simply told me, "Geri, you are a good woman, but I don't love you anymore, and I'm leaving you and getting a divorce." WHERE DID THAT COME FROM? The pit of Hell! I asked Clifton if I was a good pastor's wife and he said, "Yes, to everybody but the Pastor."

The world couldn't hold the books it would take to write all that happened that led up to that moment, or all that I went through for God to get things back where they needed to be. On the outside, we looked successful and happy. I never told a SOUL, not one, of my plight. During most of 1984, and all of 1985, I cried every single day. NO ONE ever asked me what was wrong or if I was okay. I sat on the front row of the church and cried the entire time Clifton was preaching. I guess the people must have thought I was blessed! Well, I was NOT.

Although I acted happy, and I tried to exemplify Christian joy – 'letting my light shine' – I actually felt like I might physically die over the heart-wrenching pain I was experiencing. My children noticed, but I always told them I was crying because I didn't feel good. Clifton's attitude towards them wasn't the same either, and they would come in the door and ask me, "What mood is Dad in today?" We had to walk around on eggshells. I thought perhaps the stress of the ministry was the cause of the change in Clifton. I had no idea what was really happening.

What was happening was – he thought he needed to leave us and have another life.

The God-Kind of Wife

I continued to lead the worship every service, was faithful with my responsibilities, and trusted God. I listened to Him, read my Bible, prayed and believed. As we entered our eighth year of ministry in 1984, the Lord was telling me, "Your Rose Will Bloom Again" and "New Beginnings." In the springtime of 1985, I said to God, "You are gonna have to hurry if we are getting new beginnings, because August is coming – the end of our eighth year, and things are worse than ever." THEY WERE THE WORST EVER! I don't want to sound like I was perfect. I wasn't. But I loved my husband and was determined to have God's way in our marriage, not the devil's!

I had taught a radio series called "The God Kind of Wife." I'd used Ephesians 5, Proverbs 31 and other scriptures to teach women how to be a good wife. It was the most popular teaching I ever did, and a powerful word. Literally hundreds of tapes were sent out as a result of those broadcasts. Women came from many miles to sit in my office and allow me to mentor them. I did this before, during, and after the marriage restoration.

Here's what I taught them:

- Don't treat your girlfriends better than you treat your husband.

- Honor him, whether he deserves it or not.

- Find something you can praise him for, and do it. No excuses such as "Well, if you only knew how he talks to me," etc…yada, yada.

- Carry him his coffee.

- Always have his clothes clean and in his drawers, and don't hit him the minute he comes in the door with all your negative events of the day and how bad the kids have been.

- Finally, be a doer of the Word of God.

Those are just some of the things I continued in for a very long time!

Help Arrives

August came. We had invited Andrew Wommack, a nationally known Bible teacher, to preach in a huge tent we'd rented for our celebration. One day when we took Andrew to lunch, he looked across the table at Clifton and said, "You are about to make the biggest mistake of your life." No one knew that Clifton had told our right hand man that after Andrew left, he was leaving, and he wanted all his messages on tape destroyed. Andrew invited us to his Minister's Marriage Conference in Buena Vista, Colorado. He offered to pay for the conference. All we had to do was get there.

Clifton told him we couldn't go, but I knew we were going to that meeting, come hell or high water! Clifton did say, "Well, if God provides the finances for us to get there, we'll go." It was only a month away. I packed our suitcases, and the whole time Clifton was saying he wasn't going. God performed some financial miracles and blessings, (Clifton was snared by the words of his mouth. He said he would go if the money came in!) and we were able to fly out there.

It was Heaven. That was the beginning of the turnaround. God's law of restoration is always, "Bigger, better, and more than what was lost, stolen, or taken away from you." It is always given back in better quality, quantity, and kind. I claimed that promise for my marriage. I knew God was on my side (Romans 8:31).

Now, I don't want anyone to think that this was an easy journey, because honestly, those six years were the most difficult I ever faced, and it was a minute-by-minute, hour-by-hour, and day-by-day walk with the Lord. I trusted Him to tell me what to do, what to say and how to act.

Not one person in the church knew our marriage was falling apart! I'm not saying I blame anyone, but I have felt that if the people in the church had been praying for us, it could've made a big difference. I couldn't tell anyone or seek advice, because my husband was their pastor! It was a small town. There was no one I could confide in.

God led me every step. He caused a teaching to fall into my hands which proved to be life-altering. It was about marriage and divorce, and God spoke to me that I was divorced! I was shocked. I listened further to hear Him say, "Look it up in the dictionary." The dictionary defines divorce as, "A breaking of the matrimonial bond." God began to lead me in the Scriptures, to show me things to do and say.

I never paid any attention at all to what Clifton said about getting a divorce. When he said, "I don't love you," I said, "Yes you do, you are deceived. You just think you don't love me, but really you do. You are ravished with my love!" (Proverbs 5:19) Some people would call that denial, but I call it FAITH! I never accepted any words he said to me that contradicted what the Bible said. I only believed the Word of God. It declared to me that a husband loves his wife, and is willing to give his life for her.

Clifton had been like that before his demonic "brain freeze" and he feels that way today. The restoration of our marriage was the greatest miracle I've ever seen, even though we'd seen many physical healings and miracles in the church and in our meetings. The turning of a heart is the greatest miracle ever. My rose was blooming again!

Hope Begins In Colorado

At Andrew Wommack's Minister's Marriage Conference there were a total of eight couples. Two of those were Andrew and

Jamie and a couple he had there sharing. He called me to say he was thinking of canceling the meeting. He said he'd sent out over 800 invitations to ministers and that it wasn't financially wise to rent the lodge and pay for everything for such a small group. I begged him to carry on with it. This is what I love about Andrew – he puts others first. And even though he has grown to great fame, Andrew still treats us with love, respect and affection. Andrew and his wife, Jamie, really care about people!

Every woman has to "work out her own salvation" concerning marriage and other relationships. It all boils down to listening to God; but first of all, you have to give your all to Him: be sold out, and live completely in His way and will. God did this in me. I was hopeless and helpless, but the Word of God is powerful. It is alive and it always works.

Somehow, during that marriage conference, the Holy Spirit spoke to Clifton, and God answered my prayers! We went home filled with hope and love. It was the beginning of the turnaround – but not the total fulfillment. Not yet.

As a word of encouragement, let me say this: when the Holy Spirit is leading you to do something – do it – even when it's against all odds. I could've said, "We don't have the money," or, "I don't think this will do any good." But I had heard the Lord say, "Go," and though it was a trial of huge proportions, God met me when I stepped out. He will meet you too. He is no respecter of persons. He is a respecter of faith.

The main thing is to walk in forgiveness; realize you cannot change the other person, and most of all, rely on the power of

God to work. The Bible says it does work effectually in YOU. If you believe!

The wife must, *"Do him good and not evil all the days of her life."* (Prov. 31:12) She must be Jesus in her home. A wife must put her husband first, in human relationships. That's what I did. Mostly, I followed the voice of the Holy Spirit every day. I cooked Clifton his favorite food and I told him he was ravished with my love!

Intimacy with God

After we got back to Southern Indiana and "real life," I did have a temptation to leave, but God spoke to me, "Stay put. Do not leave." So I walked the journey out totally by myself. Just me and the Holy Ghost. I learned through that dreadful experience who He is, and who I am, and I became intimate with the Lord in a fresh, incredible way.

Intimacy with God has become a major theme of my ministry. Without becoming intimate with God, we can never become what He wants us to be. We actually are already all He desires, but we don't know the amazing life He has for us until we get to know Him. I was driven to Him by my circumstances. I don't think we have to find ourselves in God this way, but it seems most do find Him through adversity.

I still thank God every day for the relationship that we developed together. He wants this with every single one of His children. I didn't say I thank Him for the problem! Some teach we should thank Him for our problems. The Bible says to thank Him *in* all things (see 1 Thessalonians 5:18), not for *all* things!

I Put My Foot Down

You know, sometimes we women just have to 'put our foot down.' Something big happened after we got back home. A couple of months had gone by and then one night Clifton woke me up from a dead sleep and announced he was leaving. A sense of righteous anger exploded inside of me, and I told him in a loud voice to "leave." "Yes," I said, "You go and take everything with you and don't ever come back!" He had a look of pure shock on his face, and he said, "What? What about the kids, what about the church? I don't want to leave." I said, "Then, do NOT ever say that to me again." And he didn't. It was a progressive healing from that moment on.

I had many friends in the church until the marriage tragedy. I lost my best friends, I was forsaken, deserted, and betrayed, but Clifton and I built back our relationship. I was more in love with my husband than ever, and he was with me, too. I missed my friends, but there was nothing I could do. They were disillusioned with my husband. They were mad at him, and that included leaving me behind also. My children lost their friends, and we were learning the loneliness of ministry. I believed we should leave the ministry, get jobs and try to be a normal family, but Clifton said he couldn't quit. So we continued to go forward with a healed marriage and a new heart. A new beginning.

It took me literally years to even speak the word 'friend.' I would be physically sick and heartsick at the mention of the word. I knew Jesus was my Friend. He spoke that to me. I read somewhere that the word friend means one who is "affectionately attached to another," and "one who sticks with you through rain or shine, thick or thin." I have found, in my many years of living life, that I can make it with Jesus and Him alone. I do love my husband, I'm devoted to my family, and I have many friends again. Even some who forsook me before have come back around, and we've picked up where we left off. But in the final analysis, it is Jesus who will never leave us, never forsake us. How I love Him!

Amazing Grace

Clifton began to preach Grace after that life-changing period of revelation and deliverance. This chapter is number five, the biblical number for GRACE. In Romans, chapter 5, verse 1 we read about having access into grace by faith. Beginning in verse 6, *"For when we were yet without strength, in due time, Christ died for the ungodly. For scarcely for a righteous man will one die, yet peradventure for a good man some would even dare to die, but God commended His love toward us, in that, while we were yet sinners, Christ died for us. Much more then, being justified by His blood, we shall be saved from wrath through Him."* As we continue to read through verses 10-20, this two-word phrase, "much more" is repeated four more times, making a total of five times we see "much more." That is grace!

Grace is a new beginning for us all. Every child of God walks in grace, not works. I was a good "works" person. I did the works. I did the "steps." But it wasn't until I understood the unmerited favor of God that I began to rest in Him. I learned that my sins were forgiven on the cross, and that was a new beginning! Now, my sins don't plague me, I have no sin as far as God is concerned (1 John 3) and as a result, I walk in a state of no sin consciousness (Hebrews 10:1).

As a final note to end this chapter, I want to say to those readers who tried to fix their marriage and ended up divorced anyway – there is no condemnation! God has a plan for everyone, and even if you are the one who messed up your life, God will take you right where you are and lead you to victory. He will give you a new beginning.

Your Rose Will Bloom Again!

Chapter 6

Cody

After God spoke to Clifton and the deception was broken, we were like newlyweds. People even said, "You two are sickening!" We were inseparable and our love grew back better than before. God kept His promises, and my husband was cooperative with the Holy Spirit. That's important, and also the fact that I didn't waver. I didn't come off of the Word of God. I listened every day, I was obedient, I didn't succumb to circumstances, but instead, I trusted in what God was telling me He would do. It was difficult, as I said, no cakewalk or trip through the proverbial tulips! Sometimes it's hard work to enter into His rest! (Hebrews 4)

Always remember the Biblical law of restoration is bigger, better, more! We had three children. After a couple years of marital bliss, we got a very big surprise. Number four – Cody! When our daughter, Kami was about 10 years old, (this was before the restoration of our marriage) she came down from upstairs and she said, "Mommy, I was praying, and God told me you are gonna have a baby before you're 40." I gasped! I said, "Oh, honey…No! Mommy is not going to have any more babies, and you shouldn't say God told you that." She was persistent, and insisted she'd heard God speak to her. During that period of time, I was fighting for my marriage. I was focused. I was consumed, actually, with saving my home and the ministry. So, I forgot all about what Kami had said.

Then one day in 1987, about four years later, I was walking with my friend Donna, at our Family and Youth Camp we'd sponsored for sixteen years, and I mentioned that my period was late (my period was never late). She said, "Let's see, if you're pregnant, you would have the baby in March. You will turn 40 in April, and Kami's prophesy is coming to pass." I was taken aback, but within a few days, I was sick in the mornings, and I'd felt that feeling before. So I knew what it was.

Now, I have to tell you, having a baby at 40 is a whole new experience! By then, our kids were 14, 16, and 19. Kelly got married in December, three months before I had the baby in March, 1988. When we told them we were having a baby, the kids were very excited, and they all took it well. I feared they'd be embarrassed. Kelly's only concern was he thought I was too old, and wanted to make sure I was going to be okay.

In my first writing of this story (around 2004) I wrote, "My kids are great, by the way." My description of Kelly was, "Our firstborn is Kelly, a tall, handsome red-headed cowboy/ construction worker." Then, I described Dustin as the manager of a sawmill supply company, but he has since started his own remodeling business. Kelly "has my coloring: red hair, light skin, blue eyes. Dustin and Kami have deep brown eyes and dark hair. They have dark completions and look like their dad."

Clifton's eyes are green, and so are Cody's; exactly like his dad's. Cody also has the same dark hair. Kelly is the only one who looked like me. He was like his dad though, in so many ways. A heart as big as the world. Cody is a mixture of all the kids. I see some of each of them in him: his personality, his expressions, his loving heart.

Many well-meaning people would say to me, "Oh, you're having a *late-life* baby," and they would look at me with pity, and sometimes I perceived disgust! One day, the Lord spoke to me and said, "This is not a late-life baby. This is a baby born in due season for such a time as this, and he will be a restorer of life to you, and a joy to help you in your old age." (As I write this, I am reminded that Kelly always told us he would be the one to take care of us when we needed taking care of in our old age. His wife Darlene was all for it too and we'd planned to live with them, or have a small place of our own on their property). I never realized until recently how vital that promise was, how important, and how certainly we never knew that we would face his untimely death before he faced our need for care. Life doesn't always turn out as we plan. Or does it ever?

To make matters worse, I would see the buttons and refrigerator magnets that said, "I'd rather be 40 than pregnant!" I was 40 AND pregnant and it felt like the world wanted to double curse me. I never received any of it though. People would say, "I'm glad that it's you and not me." I finally heard it so much I started saying, "I'm glad it's me too. Children are a gift from God!" I was receiving this baby as a gift.

An Unexpected Guest

The pregnancy wasn't easy. I was extremely sick most of the time. I claimed every day that I wasn't under the curse. I read a book on how to have natural childbirth – with no pain, and I was really into it. Clifton and I took the Lamaze classes. We were excited to have this baby!

During my pregnancy, something else was happening at our house. My mother-in-law, Ferne, lived on our property. She had announced one Christmas a few years before that she had some bad news for me. I said, "What is it?" She said, "I am buying a house trailer and putting it on your property." We were thrilled. She had lived with all her other children except us.

So, we cleared her out a spot across the driveway, and we placed her home in the midst of the dogwood trees. Clifton made her a flower bed. The kids helped her get everything organized and it was pure joy. After a year or so, she said, "Geri, this is the happiest I've ever been in my life." Wow! She also told me one day, "Geri, I find no fault in you." I nearly fell down! I was good to her, we got along famously. I cut her hair, gave her perms, took her to Louisville to the doctor, and anything else I could do. The kids treated her great too, and she bragged on them to me.

Something is Wrong with Mammaw

About the time I was so sick with the pregnancy, she became ill too. She'd been supernaturally healed of cancer, but her doctor wanted to make sure the cancer didn't come back, and so he'd put her on some preventative chemotherapy pills. I would send the kids over to check on her because I was in bed, throwing up. One day, Kami came in and said, "Something is wrong with Mammaw Coulter." She said Ferne was saying her words wrong, so I hurried over there and realized she hadn't been to bed and was talking in an incoherent manner.

I called her daughter, Mary Ann, who was a nurse and lived in Louisville. She came up from Louisville to help. Ferne's legs were swollen, and in the end, we discovered her brain had swollen also: a side effect of the medication. The other siblings wanted to place her in a nursing home because both daughters worked. One son was an OTR (over-the-road) truck driver and the other son lived in Florida. Clifton said, "No nursing home," so we brought her into our home and between Clifton, me and the kids, we took care of her until she died.

Our church people had experience bathing the elderly, and they helped us too. They sat with her when I needed to go to town for groceries or errands. What a blessing. Then, Mary Ann had a nine day vacation, and she and her husband came and picked Ferne up and took her to their home. She was going to return, but instead, Ferne passed on the last day of her visit. The time Ferne spent in our home was a precious, treasured time. I thank God for it, because Clifton had no guilt about his mother afterwards. Here's an amazing thing: I didn't throw up at all from the time Ferne came to live in our home until the November night when she passed away.

A Blessing Arrives

Now it was 1988 and the eights were double. New Beginnings
– bigger, more, better than before! That's what the Lord
brought us.

On March 16, my water was leaking, so the doctor put me in
the hospital. My mom came out, and we were all excited that
the baby would be born on her birthday. WRONG! I went in
around noon, and he wasn't born until 24 hours later. By the
way, the books on "no pain in childbirth" didn't work for me.
The labor pains were horrendous and the transition experience
was brand new, as I'd had medication to numb the feeling of
childbirth with my other three children. Pain! The nausea lasted
until the baby was born.

It was St Patrick's Day, so we named him Cody Patrick. Now
we had three teenagers and a newborn. It was wild! (Kelly was
married by this time, but we had another teen living in our
home, so I still had three teenagers.) I wanted to name Cody
Isaac Nathaniel. To this day, you can ask him what his spiritual
name is and what it means, and he will tell you "laughter" and
"one without bitterness or guile." I can honestly say that Cody
has always made us laugh, and he has absolutely no bitterness,
at all, towards anyone; even when he's been treated badly.

Cody has been a blessing, truly a gift from God, although he
marches to a very different drummer than our other children.
He loves God and loves us, and we have great hope for his
future. He's more creative, more the 'outside the box' type
than our other kids; or was it that we wouldn't allow the older
kids to be as creative as they desired? I'm ashamed to say that

we were too strict and narrow-minded when it came to raising our older children. By the time Cody was growing up, the others were married and out of the house. We were too tired to crack the whip like we did with the first three! Smile.

Chapter 7

New Adventures in Ministry

Here we are at Chapter seven. The number seven is God's number for completion and we were about to complete a season of our life and ministry.

Before Cody was one year old, Clifton accepted an invitation to go to India. This is a miraculous story. We had met C.P. Thomas, the Indian national, about a year earlier through another friend, Daryl Holloman. We had first helped raise money for Daryl to go to India. He ended up not going at that time, but had given C.P. the idea he was coming, and C.P. didn't know Daryl had canceled the trip. So, when we said Clifton was coming, and bringing Kenny Gerry (a longtime friend who Clifton had asked to make the trip with him), C.P. wasn't sure, even though we sent a telegram saying they would arrive on February 2.

We gave the name of the airline and exact time of arrival, but C.P. wasn't at the airport. Clifton was expecting C.P. to pick him up and take it from there, so he didn't even know the name of the town where C.P. was. (We later learned that C.P. lived seven and a half hours away, by jeep, from the city of Cochin, where the plane had landed.) You would need to hear Clifton tell this story, because it is hilarious (well, it was funny – later.) At the time, it was a nightmare! No C.P. at the airport and Clifton spoke NO Hindi. He barely speaks English!

Revival!

Cochin was packed with what seemed like millions of Indians. Finally, Clifton remembered that another missionary who had gone over to India had stayed at the Queen Mary Hotel in Cochin. A taxi driver took them there. Clifton asked about C.P. Thomas, and surprisingly the hotel attendant knew him, and pulled up his name and phone number, which was 97. Yes, 97. Clifton told the little guy to call C.P., and he said, "No, he could not call C.P." He said he would have to send a telegram instead. For Clifton, that was not going to do. Clifton INSISTED (a nice way to say it), that C.P. be called on the telephone. The hotel attendant kept saying, "You don't understand," and my husband said, "No, YOU don't understand." So, Clifton and Kenny got a room, went up and laid down, and the phone on the wall rang. It was C.P., who kept repeating, "Oh, Pastor, this is a great miracle!" Clifton says the miracle was that he didn't strangle C.P.

The MIRACLE actually was this: There were NO PHONE LINES from Cochin to the village of Nedakkandam, down south on the edge of the jungle. The 97 was a village number. Only the villagers could use that system!

So, Ronald Dennison, C.P.'s son, drove the seven and a half hours through the night to pick up Clifton and Kenny in Cochin. C.P. said he wasn't at the airport because we didn't have the year on the telegram. February 2nd of what year? (We sent the telegram in January, 1989.)

Because of that initial move (the miracle) of God, C.P. was excited above measure! Every time he came to one of our churches, he preached on this as one of the greatest miracles that ever happened in his ministry. He's been to Missouri twice over the past few years and C. P. says Clifton is the greatest man of God he knows!

Since C.P. didn't know they were coming, and there was a huge political rally in the village, there were no jeeps available to rent to get out to the jungle – to the natives, the nomads, and the tribal people. These folks were the focus of C.P.'s ministry.

Clifton was to be there for thirty days, so he lit a fire under C.P. to get some people together. They found a makeshift tent and stretched it between two buildings. The revival meetings began and people came. When the Americans arrived, C.P. had about 28 people in his little church, but by the time Clifton and Kenny left, C.P. had over 200 people in church and needed larger facilities! His ministry has now grown into the thousands, and C.P. has over a hundred churches scattered across India. His son, Ronald Dennison, is a pastor too.

Miracles in India

There were tremendous miracles during that trip and every trip afterwards. I will share a few. There was a man named Siva Das, meaning "healing god" in Hindi. He was paralyzed from his waist up, and couldn't move his arms. He was a beggar. He was completely healed in the second meeting they had in

Nedakkandam. There was a write-up in the Indian national newspaper with C.P., Clifton, Kenny, and Siva Das on the front page with Siva Das' story. The next time Clifton went over to India, Siva Das had a truck driving job. Siva had been a beggar his whole life, until Jesus showed up!

The second most miraculous thing (to me), that happened on that trip, was the healing of a man who had no sight. His eyes were bluish-white balls; no color in them at all. The guys prayed for him, and the next night there was no small stir when the man came to the meeting, completely healed, with two perfect eyes – black as the rest of the people there! There were also deaf and dumb children healed who spoke and could hear the "selfsame" night!

But here is the most amazing thing! We received a letter of commendation from the Indian government to the Lighthouse (and Clifton Coulter, Kenny Gerry and C.P. Thomas) for extinguishing the marijuana business on the mountain! Clifton and Kenny had no idea it was a drug-infested mess there, or that the government was watching that area closely. The Indian government said after the Americans had been there, all the marijuana was cut down and burned by the people who lived on the mountain. They all turned to Jesus!

A witch came to one of the meetings, and C.P. didn't want to deal with her, so he told Clifton to leave her alone because she was trouble. But the Holy Spirit led Clifton to minister to her, and Clifton had a word of knowledge about her heart. He didn't know her leg was stiff too, but when he prayed for her, she slid down the wall, knees up to her chest. The next morning, before daylight, she knocked on C.P.'s door to tell him she was completely healed, and wanted this Jesus they were talking about! She invited them to her home, and had dozens of people there waiting to get saved! They all came to C.P.'s church after that.

Later, Clifton took a team from the Lighthouse over to India, and made another trip with Kevin Lauritsen after we moved to Colorado. We have video of some of this. How amazing!

A Financial Miracle

One elderly American woman supplied the guys with most of the finances to go on the trip. We raised money, over a thousand dollars, through our church and our radio partners, to give to C.P. as an offering for his ministry in India. Our church had no money in any accounts to just automatically provide for an overseas trip. Another miracle that happened was that while Pastor Clifton was gone for those thirty days, our church finances went down the drain. My treasurer/secretary, Shirley Cornelison (later Ferrell), came into my office one day and laid down a stack of bills on my desk and said, "If we don't get seven thousand dollars in here, quick, we're going to have to shut the doors!" My heart sank. I was panicked on the inside, but I calmly said, "No, we won't." I laid my hands on those bills and made her do it too, and we prayed.

Two days before Clifton was to return home, I was at our house and answered the phone to hear a friend saying, "I was backing out of my driveway, and God spoke to me to send your church 5,000 dollars, and to send you 5,000 dollars!"

Once again, God showed Himself to be Who He says He is: our provider, Jehovah Jireh! Clifton knew nothing of our financial crunch. He was only able to call me once in thirty days, and C.P. had to drive him nearly a hundred miles to get to a telephone.

When Ellen and I went to pick up the guys at the airport, I wasn't just a little tickled to be able to tell him about the finances and our miracle. Clifton said, "Well, God didn't send me halfway around the world so I could come back home and fail."

Around that time, we began to be get invitations to travel and preach. We didn't call anyone and ask, "Can we come?" Soon, our schedule was full all the time. We were having a blast after our marriage was healed, and the offerings were abundant in our evangelistic ministry.

Goodbye to Our Baby, Our Precious Lighthouse

By 1994, the Lord had been speaking to Clifton (for two years) about going on the road full-time and giving up the church. We were already traveling three weekends out of the month, and had placed four men in charge of the church to cover for us, and to lead the church in our absence. We kept in close contact with them, and still remained the senior pastors. Clifton and I loved that church, and I felt like the "mother" of the church, and the people. I couldn't let go of it. When Clifton would tell me his heart's desire – that he wanted to leave the church – I just couldn't accept it. However, as I sought the Lord's will, I felt the time was coming. We solicited a couple who we thought could take over as pastors of the church but they wouldn't do it. They prayed about it, and didn't feel led to do it. We had met with them and told them of the financial situation, which wasn't widely known (that being, that Clifton and I sacrificed our all to keep the doors open on the church. It was our vision, it was our life. We could find no one willing to pay the price. I don't mean to "boast" or sound like we want to be applauded, I'm just saying how it was).

One Sunday, Clifton was preaching, and he said, "This is my last Sunday here as pastor of this church." I was sitting on the front row, and nearly fell onto the floor. But, that was it.

We had started, or "pioneered" the church in 1977 with a handful of people, and had grown it to over 300 at one time, between 1977 and 1984. In 1984, we made the move to the country, near Hardinsburg, not knowing that some of the people wouldn't be going with us. We needed more room, and had expanded as much as we possibly could where we were. There was simply no parking, and no way to expand. We'd purchased property and a building in Marengo, Indiana to house our school. The two pieces of property we bought in Hardinsburg would be big enough for our church and school. The payments were high though, and that is the reason Clifton didn't want to receive money from the church as a salary.

The treasurer had set an allowance of $125 per week for our basic needs. This went on until 1988. Now, when I say $125 per week, I mean that is ALL. No salary, no benefits, no gas money, NOTHING but the $125 per week! I have often wondered what the people thought. They knew we had no secular income, and they knew we didn't receive much from the church, yet we were raising three kids and had a $600.00 month house payment plus the electric bill, phone bill, etc.

We preached strong faith, and God did take care of us, but it wasn't primarily through the church people. It was outside people for the most part. God would speak to people to go and pay bills for us, and many times people would drive to our home and bring envelopes full of money, hundreds of dollars. Each time they said God had spoken to them to do this.

We NEVER told one person about our lack. We never one time said we didn't have something. We knew those who did that, and we always said to each other that they got stuff given to them because people felt sorry for them. If anyone found out that we had a need, it would be because they had come to our home, and had seen that we were out of something. I remember, once I had been without a cook stove for six months. I cooked on a hot plate and a "deep fryer." There were no crock pots or microwaves back then, or if there were any microwaves, we sure didn't have one!

One day, a man from the church came by and saw I had no stove, and he went immediately and got one, brought it to me and hooked it up! I didn't complain, because I never felt I was in lack! I just did whatever I had to do. Honestly, we never acted in lack. We preached prosperity so strong that I guess everyone thought we were fine. And we were. Smile.

I know this is hard to believe, and when I think back on it, I feel stupid and naive. However, at the time, we were absolutely thrilled to have been called by God and entrusted with such a call, and we knew God would take care of everything. We were filled with FAITH! I can honestly say that neither Clifton nor I ever did anything in ministry for money.

"God Will Have to Take Care of You"

One time, an evangelist called us to come to Florida and do some teachings on marriage during the morning sessions of his tent revival. We paid our own way; he had us a place to stay (with a family), and we did our meetings. He told us, however, we'd have to receive our own offerings. This was around 1990, and we had never received our own offering anywhere we'd ever preached, and Clifton told him we couldn't do that. Clifton said, "God will take care of us." So, the evangelist set a basket out and told the people to put something in it for us. He took us to lunch (he was older than we were) and talked to us about our teachings. He said (speaking of our "Marriage Encounter" teachings), "You have a gold mine here." He started counseling us on how to receive offerings and how to get the people to give, but we said we couldn't do it. He finally got aggravated with us and said, "God will have to take care of you, because you sure don't know how to take care of yourselves." He was mad!

Clifton and I laughed. God has always taken care of us. All that time as pastors, we had no money, but we never lost anything, never had our electricity or phone cut off; everything was supernaturally paid. We never missed a meal. That went on for years, in fact, the whole seventeen years we were pastoring at the Lighthouse.

Something else miraculous happened on that trip to Florida. While we were on the plane traveling there, the Lord spoke to me. He said, "A classy lady is going to bless you." After I got to Florida, I forgot all about it. For one thing, we were having the tent meetings next door to an old-time Pentecostal church, and (I don't want to sound snotty, but) I saw no classy looking ladies!

Then one day, a woman was going into the church to give a piano lesson, and she saw us and came over to the tent. She stayed for the Marriage Encounter sessions, and was so excited she could hardly contain herself. She needed marriage help! The next day, she came with a box and inside the box was a linen suit. It was beautiful and lavender colored. The following morning, she came with a silk blouse, a silk purple suit, and a black silk skirt! She had gone to New York (Bloomingdales' suppliers), and purchased the clothes to resell to her friends in Florida, but she said she needed to sow some seed, and the Lord told her to give me the clothes. The price tag on just the blouse was $250! I was crazy about those clothes! I would never have spent the money, even if I had plenty, on clothes for myself. My Father God, isn't He amazing? I wore the purple silk suit to teach one of my CBC sessions (Colorado Bible College) on "The Virtuous Woman." My students raved!

You Can't Out Give God

This same evangelist came to our church one September for a revival. A woman from our church had given me a 100 dollar bill and told me to go shopping because she knew we were headed to Colorado for Andrew Wommack's Minister's

Conference. I kept the money in my purse. I'd taken the evangelist's wife shopping, but I didn't find anything I wanted, so I didn't spend my money. The last night of the meetings, the preacher said, "Now, the Lord is speaking to me to have you place your biggest bill in an envelope and write on it what you are sowing for."

Here's a little lesson: no one can out give God. That is not just a manipulative saying used by preachers to get money out of people. I've heard all the excuses of why people don't give to the church, or to preachers. Clifton and I have tithed to the church since the day we heard it taught at the Baptist Church, when we first got saved. Back then, we had twenty dollars to our name, and Clifton was laid off from work, yet he put it in the offering! We have always given way beyond our ability to give and our lives are a testimony of the faithfulness of God. He did say that we should give, and it would be given unto us (Luke 6:23). Jesus did teach on tithing, even in the gospels. Jesus told them they gave tithes of their spices (Matthew 23:23), but left out the more important things (neglected the weightier matters): justice, mercy, and faith. Then He said, "*These things you ought to have done, without leaving the others undone.*"

The evangelist handed out envelopes for us to put our biggest bill in, and write on it what we were sowing for. I don't even remember what I wrote, but I do remember sealing the envelope with my tears! (Figuratively.) I wasn't happy. I was not a cheerful giver that night. However, that very week, a friend called and wanted us to drive to Louisville to meet him for dinner. He said he wanted to write us a check; he said he thought it would be about $3,000, but when we got there to have dinner, he wrote it for $5,000! "Sister Coulter," you might ask, "are you saying God gave you $5,000 because you gave that $100 out of obedience?" YES, without a doubt!

Finances in Ministry

I do wish Clifton had continued working his superintendent job in the early days of our ministry, but we felt compelled to be free to talk to people day and night about the Lord and the Holy Spirit. Andrew Wommack gives the testimony that when he first started ministering he had this mindset: that a called man of God could not work secular work. At the time, we considered it a lack of faith.

Eleven years after we started the Lighthouse, we received a raise to $150 per week and after that, a group of new people came in from the Baptist church and convinced our board to pay our house payment, electricity, and phone. What a huge blessing! Before this, we were standing in faith and believing for every single house payment, and every bill, even groceries. It took a lot of money to raise three kids, then four.

One day I was praying for money and God spoke very clearly to my spirit. He said, "You don't need money." That was early in our ministry. Kelly needed shoes and books for school. Our tires were thread bare. In fact, wires were sticking out, and we just prayed and kept going for Jesus! After that prayer, a man we had known from the Baptist church came by with four brand new tires that fit our car, and he dropped them beside the driveway, and called later to tell us what he'd done. A family member (who'd never previously been one to donate to us or our ministry) took Kelly and bought his school shoes and paid for his books. Someone came while we were gone and filled our refrigerator and cabinets with food, and left money under my table centerpiece. (This happened several times). We had not said ONE WORD to anyone about our situation! It was then that I understood what the Lord meant: we didn't need money, all we needed was faith!

We preached faith as good as anyone! It was a strong faith message. The problem was; we weren't always living it like it should've been lived! Sometimes, we were so poor we couldn't even buy a Coke after church. Those were difficult times, but to tell you the truth, we didn't notice. I can remember wrapping up a picture of a gift one of the kids wanted for their birthday. (We would eventually get the money and get them what they wanted, but many times they had to wait.) We always had a party though – cake, ice cream, and family! I would take the one having the special day out for the entire afternoon and we would go somewhere. I've continued that practice with my grandchildren too.

God Meets Our Needs

I used to bake a lot of bread. We took it out to give to people, and then invite them to our "Bread of Life" Thanksgiving services. One time, an elderly gentleman gave me a fifty pound bag of flour because I'd given him a loaf of bread. Then the grocer, who had a small store within walking distance of our home, offered me the privilege of buying his cases of canned goods for 25 cents over cost, so I purchased a case of applesauce. I shall never forget (nor shall my family), the time we had no money for food and the cabinets were bare. I never said a word to my kids (or in front of them) about our lack. Instead, I went to my big bag of flour and baked bread. I opened the applesauce, and served that for breakfast one morning. Everyone loved it! Lunch time came, and I served it again. That night, we had homemade bread and applesauce for supper.

The next morning, I baked cinnamon bread, and you guessed it, applesauce! By the fourth or fifth day, my kids finally began to moan a little. "Again?" they asked.

None of us ever said a word to a living soul. One day, when we were gone from our home, someone was sensitive to the Lord and brought us groceries like we'd never seen! That was another time when the freezer, refrigerator, and cabinets were all full to overflowing when we returned. And that's just one of the examples of how God met our needs, and took care of us for years.

As we began to accept invitations to go out and preach, our income grew. I remember those first offerings were hundreds, even thousands of dollars! God was speaking that this is what He wanted for us. People accepted us, and by that time, Clifton was preaching the Grace of God and His unconditional love, not what all we have to do to get God's attention.

After we actually resigned the church, I felt a ton of weight come off my chest. I didn't even know it had been there. I never realized how stressed I was about the church, paying for the property, the care of the people. I'd carried the burden of the payments almost entirely by myself for ten years. It felt good to be free. We worked with each family to help them relocate to another church in the area. People had been coming to the Lighthouse from a 70-mile radius, which was major in those days, but other churches had sprung up by then, and there were places to go, besides our church, to hear the truth.

After we resigned from the Lighthouse in 1994, I was offered a position on a live television broadcast, "Prayer and Praise." It was a 30-minute segment where I was to receive calls on the air and answer questions. Between calls, I was encouraged, by the station owner, to teach from the Bible. It was a glorious year there at the station. We traveled; I did the TV show and took care of Cody.

Before we'd resigned from the Lighthouse, Clifton was offered a teaching position at CBC (Colorado Bible College, now Charis Bible College), Andrew Wommack's Bible college, for the 1995-96 school year, so that whole year of traveling ministry was preparation to move to Colorado.

By the time we moved, we had pastored for seventeen years and been on the road full-time for a year. But we left it all: our dream home of eighteen years, our family, and our friends, and moved to Colorado.

Our rose was about to bloom in the Colorado Mountains!

Chapter 8

Colorado

It's ironic that this is Chapter 8 because eight is God's number for New Beginnings. Yes, we definitely got a new beginning in Colorado in many ways. First of all, I want to tell you, that, as much as it hurt me to leave my kids and grandkids in Indiana, I knew that God had something for us that would be life changing. I knew this was a call from God, an assignment, not just an invitation from Andrew Wommack, whom we loved and would've done anything for. I knew this would be a time of healing for Clifton and me. There were some painful, heart breaking memories about the marriage falling apart (and the effect it had on our family) that I wanted to leave in Indiana. I'd prayed for God to do something to help. The move was our answer.

Heaven on Earth

Clifton's brother, Ivan, was a professional truck driver and he brought his 18-wheeler up from Texas all the way to our home, loaded our stuff, and moved us to Manitou Springs, Colorado. We'd made a trip out there in June and found a perfect home. God had told me one day, while we were still in Indiana and I was lamenting leaving my beautiful home, "I am going to give you a WOW house." God outdid Himself with the way He provided for us, and we also had favor with the manager of the place. It was perfect.

That house was the most awesome home I'd ever lived in! It was a Spanish style, tri-level with a mountaintop view that overlooked Red Rock Canyon and a national forest. When I came down the stairs each morning, the first thing that I saw was my own view of Pike's Peak. Right out my front door. I could see the Garden of the Gods from my kitchen window, and at night our view was the lights of Colorado Springs. Heaven on earth? Absolutely.

We were five minutes from the Bible College, where our office was located. Many mornings, as I drove down the mountain to work, I had tears of joy running down my face as I thought about the awesomeness of God and His loving provision. I was the happiest I'd ever been!

Of course, I missed my kids, but we were being used of God and they understood that and had encouraged us to go. We met many new and wonderful people and made some lifelong relationships.

A Promise Comes to Pass

I want to share a story here that illustrates the faithfulness of God and His ability to show us things to come. Back in the early 1980's, when Clifton was telling me that "he didn't love me and wanted a divorce," we'd taken a trip on our motorcycle to visit friends in Florida. I woke up real early one morning and went into their beautiful kitchen to read my Bible.

That morning the Lord took me into the Old Testament. He took me there supernaturally. I couldn't remember ever having read the verse before. It was Habakkuk 3:17-19: *Though the fig tree may not blossom, Nor fruit be on the vines; Though the labor of the olive may fail, And the trees yield no food; Though the flock be cut off from the fold, And there be no herd in the stalls – Yet I will rejoice in the Lord, I will joy in the God of my salvation. The Lord God is my strength; He will make my feet like deer's feet, And He will make me walk on my high hills.*

Years later, in 1995 when we were settled in Colorado, I wrote one morning in my Bible that I was truly walking on high hills, and I wept at the faithfulness of God to me personally. His promise to me that Florida morning, so many years ago, had come to pass!

I certainly had no fig tree blossoming during the time when God gave me that scripture in their beautiful kitchen. My tree was dead in those days. The marriage had fallen apart and I didn't know what to do. But God – God will meet you right where you are, and use words (His Word), written centuries ago, to speak to you. His Word will give you direction, and He will use it to make sure promises to you.

Don't Quit

In those days, I was living one minute at a time, listening with all my heart to the voice of the Holy Spirit. Then, twelve years later, here I was living in Colorado and enjoying what God had promised.

I can tell you this: too many times people give up, quit, and don't allow the fruit of the Spirit to manifest. Anyone who has Jesus has the patience needed to stand, and having done all to stand (see Ephesians 6:13). I praised the Lord *anyway* during those critical years. Yes, I said *years*, about six of them to be exact.

There were good times intermingled, but for the most part I felt alone and struggling; I wasn't able to confide in a living soul. I got to know my Heavenly Father, the work of the Holy Spirit, and the love of my Savior, Jesus Christ. I started learning what it meant to *rejoice always* (see Philippians 4:4), and *to count it all joy when you fall into different trials and temptations* (see James 1:2). That means: rejoice when you don't feel like it! These are some real big keys to the Christian life: be thankful for what you have and don't look at what you don't have.

Clifton was the one who was offered the instructor position at Colorado Bible College, so I stayed home and got my house in order. I didn't realize how tired I was until we got moved. I'd driven 100 miles a day the whole year before we moved: driving 25 miles to take Cody to a private Christian school, doing my TV broadcast, driving 25 miles back home, then the 50 mile round-trip to pick up Cody in the afternoon. That, plus all the ministry travel we'd done on a regular basis, had left me physically exhausted.

So, I enjoyed working and decorating my new home. My furniture matched the carpet and colors in the home, and I'd always wanted a certain kind of hardwood floor, and there it was – in the foyer, dining room and kitchen. Also, for years I'd asked Clifton to build me some window sills in our home so I could put lights in the windows. This house had marble windowsills throughout, and I was thrilled to finally be able to buy a bunch of candles and place them in every window in the house. It was so much fun!

Teacher, Teacher

Everything was perfect. I began to make friends. I was also getting to fill in occasionally for Clifton at the Bible college. I was so excited because the students at that time were mostly female and the school realized their need for a woman teacher, so eventually, I was asked to become an instructor too.

I'd hosted many women's conferences in Indiana over my pastoral tenure, so I began to host them in Colorado as well. One of the students, Deanne Sarah, became my greatest supporter. She helped us in the office, and we went places together. We knew each other's heart. She told me I was thinking too small about the first ladies meeting we were planning. I'd rented a room that seated 20 and she said, "No, 40." She was right.

Deanne said in the beginning that her husband Rick would love Clifton, so we all got together and, sure enough, they hit it off. "Friends for life," she said. We're still friends with Rick Sarah, but Deanne was killed in a tragic head-on car accident, shortly after graduating from CBC. She and Rick had been in our home for lunch the Sunday before the Thursday accident. She was the closest friend I had ever lost like that. I actually had a dream that she was in Heaven and wouldn't come back if she could. Her sudden, unexpected death was heart wrenching for us all. Clifton and Andrew did the funeral at a large church in Colorado Springs and 500 people attended the service. Many were born again.

Rick got a new beginning when God sent him a beautiful woman, Chris, who loved him. They got married and even had a baby at a more advanced age than Clifton and me when we had Cody. They named the child Shiloh. What a tremendous blessing and gift from God! If we will just look to our Heavenly Father, whether we understand things or not, He will sweep in and save the day for anyone. His love is higher than the mountains, even higher than Pike's Peak.

Hard Times in High Places

Our time in Colorado was bittersweet. God used us in many miraculous ways. As time has passed, I've chosen to only remember the super, awesome relationships we developed, the wonderful people we met, and how those connections changed our lives.

The day we arrived in Colorado, we met someone connected with the school who, it seemed to us, had an agenda – an agenda to immediately get rid of us. From our perspective (and with good reason), there were signs of insecurity and this person had the authority to make our lives miserable at times. The entire (almost) four years were the most awesome, incredible, and amazing period of time in our ministry, while at the same time, we endured heartbreaking persecution. Andrew traveled a lot and he didn't know about the problem until we were ready to leave the Bible college. We were determined not to complain, because everything else was so wonderful.

At the same time the individual was causing us grief, there were out-of-this-world blessings and we loved the work we were doing. One night, I was asked to teach a Bible study at one of the apartment community rooms where there were many students and nations represented. I thought it was Heaven! God began to use me in a new way in the gifts of the Holy Spirit. Every person I touched in prayer, I saw a picture of their lives, and what God was fixing to do in their lives. I'd received a prophetic word a few days earlier that God wanted to stretch me like a rubber band. The word had been that God wanted me to step out in some gifts that were inside me. To this day, those gifts continue to come forth. That word and the Bible study were rose blooming experiences because, although I'd been used in the gifts before, for some reason, I'd allowed myself to be shut down over the past few years.

Lights...Camera...Action!

While I was teaching, the students in attendance were learning the media part of ministry and practicing by videoing my classes. I didn't remember even noticing that they were doing it, so I never dressed for filming or planned my classes for video. I just went in, taught, was myself, and enjoyed to the max every single minute.

One day, someone on staff came to me and said, "Geri, we are preparing our videoed classes for the CBC Correspondence School, and one of our teachers failed to turn on his microphone, so there's no audio on his course. Would you consider letting us use yours? Your teachings are the only other ones we have on video." Now, I cannot tell you the sense I had on the inside of me. Would I consider it? Really? My insides were doing cartwheels and jumping jacks, but I calmly said, "Yes, of course."

So, my courses on *The Book of Ruth* and *Proverbs* literally went all over the world for years. When I would go to England, Ireland, or Scotland, the ladies (and some guys too) would come to me and want pictures with me, since they'd been enrolled in the CBC Correspondence classes. Some comments I got were that, "they were so happy to have a woman along with the men teachers," One lady wrote me and said, "You are the chocolate chips in the cookies."

Our income soared because of the connections we made. We traveled and preached every weekend. We toured in the summer, traveling so much that Cody cried one day when we stopped by home for a couple days to unpack, repack, and start again. He was six to ten years old while we lived in Colorado.

Clifton was greatly loved by the students. We had them over to our home to eat Thanksgiving and Christmas dinners when we were in town. Many had no place to go. They were from Germany, Switzerland, England, Scotland, Africa, and other places. We also had some students living with us, because we had three bathrooms and plenty of room.

So, except for the person who leveled false accusations against us and appeared to have an agenda of eliminating us from the school, everything else was so great. It was like a dream world. Our time there was the most memorable, prosperous, and anointed time of our entire lives. Andrew and Jamie were, and continue to be, wonderful people, full of integrity and love. Andrew came to our church to dedicate our newly purchased building in 2013, and to this day, Clifton and Andrew have a deep, brotherly affection for each other.

A Great Battle

Clifton went through a physical battle, for his very life, a few months before we left Colorado. The doctor said that stress was likely the root because there was no reason for the illness, medically speaking. They call it idiopathic when they can't find a medical explanation. The stress caused a pancreatic shutdown: a disease known as Pancreatitis. We spent four months in and out of the hospital and home care. Three specialists in Colorado Springs told me, after Clifton was healed, that they'd been very worried about my husband. They thought, "He was gonna die," and so did Clifton's sister, who, by this time, had been a nurse for over forty years.

It started at the end of the 1998 school year. We normally weren't paid in the summer, and we couldn't travel and preach because of Clifton's illness, so we had zero income. During that summer, Clifton wasn't allowed a single bite of food for 80 days. He was fed by a bag of parenteral nutrition that was pumped into his veins by a special machine (which I was trained to hook up) for twelve hours a day. He also got a bag of saline, and a bag of antibiotics for up to eight hours a day. I used a needle and shot vitamins and medicine into the bags. When I look back, it seems impossible to me that we got through this. We were mostly alone. Cody was just ten. Those who came to visit were treasures. By this time, we were buying a five-acre mini ranch and lived an hour out from the Springs. It was a lonely time, but a time of trusting God's Word.

God Proves Himself Faithful

Here's what God did: before anyone even knew of our situation or that Clifton was in the hospital, we received a check in the mail for $800. It was sent by a set of twin boys who'd listened to Clifton's teachings for their home school chapel time. They were only ten years old. The check was some of the money they'd earned, working on their parents' farm.

I received some other money as well, and I took it and showed it to Clifton. When I went to the mailbox and saw the checks, I said," God, this is a miracle!" He immediately spoke to my heart, "This is not a miracle, this is a result of your seed sown over the years." He also reminded me of the twelve cars we'd given away, the times we'd given when we had nothing left; the times we'd sown into people lives.

I realized then that this is how the Father takes care of His kids. We shall be forever grateful to Don Krow, who asked me for our ministry mailing list. He sent out a brief message about Clifton to everyone on our list. We received a $2,000 check by Federal Express overnight, from a friend down in Texas. I remember one of the ministries we supported sent us money and were in awe that we were still sending our monthly support to them.

Well, yes we did, thanks be to God. He always provides seed for the sower (see 2 Corinthians 9:10). We received a total of

$48,000 that summer. Because we had no insurance and no income, there was some grant money available through the hospital, which was applied to our bill; all without us even asking for a thing.

Also, one night we drove up into the mountains to hear Andrew, and he announced that his offering that evening would be going directly to us. Who else does that? All the medical bills were PAID by the end of that tragic, seemingly hopeless, illness. Our rose was crushed, but then it bloomed again! New Beginnings.

We saw miracles concerning Clifton's health every time we turned around. Sometimes we were asked, "What about healing for Clifton?" Folks were thinking of all the healings we'd witnessed and wondering about how that applied to Clifton's illness. Well, the end-result was that he was healed. We mustn't give up, or look at present circumstances, but rather, have hope in God. (see Psalms 42:5)

In the hospital, Jesus came into Clifton's room and stood beside the bed. Clifton's testimony is that he felt this Presence, but dared not open his eyes. The message he received from the Lord was to never allow anyone to get between them again. Other hospital visitors were Andrew Wommack, Dave and Bonnie Duell, Don Francisco, Paul Wilbur, many of the students, and of course, Wendell and Linda Parr, Johnna and Chuck Smith, and our good friends, Dennis and Denise Capra. Kevin Lauritsen came the 35 miles out to Calhan on the prairie to see us at the ranch. So did Greg Troup and Kim Williams.

Also, while we were still living in Colorado, our daughter and her husband moved out there, and Kami had her first baby, Taylor LeeAnne. They moved back to Indiana when the baby was nine months old. I've been so blessed, I've been present for all my grandkid's births. I gave each one their first bath. (I'm one of those grandmothers!)

In January 1999, when our season was over at CBC, we chose to move back home. "Back home to Indiana," as the old song goes. I cried until there were no more tears. It was a devastating loss to leave my students and the school. There was a going away party, planned by our friends (it was a large, packed out meeting room at a hotel) where Clifton spoke. Folks sang to us, and I was given a large bouquet of yellow roses, my favorite!

I couldn't see how we would ever have a better new beginning than what we'd been involved with those past few years in Colorado, so it was a sad time for me. I went onto auto-pilot for a bit. We stayed in Colorado for a little while and then headed back home.

Chapter 9

Back Home Again in Indiana

We left the Bible school in January and moved back to Indiana in April of 1999. I wanted to be around my family. I was devastated and I couldn't get a grip on what had happened. I felt my rose was dead. My heart was dead. I didn't want to teach. I didn't want to do anything. For the first time in my life, my joy was gone. Even in the past, when Clifton had threatened to leave me, (I never believed it) I had a supernatural hope and faith that God had spoken to me and I knew things would be okay.

This time was different. I heard nothing from God. We moved into my son's house. I went to bed at 6 p.m. and stayed there till morning. I didn't want to talk to anyone. Clifton took me to funny movies and tried his best, but nothing helped. I couldn't get over it.

Clifton's perspective was that he was excited. The Lord had spoken to him while we were still in Colorado to go east and surround himself with young men to mentor and train up for ministry. He was to use his wisdom and experience and they were to furnish the youth, the energy.

One day I was sitting on the porch feeling sad, and the phone rang. It was my good friend, Shirley Osborne. She had picked up on my spiritual condition, and she just began to pour life into me. She said, "Geri, you are anointed, you are valuable to God, and He is gonna use you again, and you'll be happy, and have a greater ministry than ever before." and on and on she went. Somehow, I started to believe her.

A New Church, Again

Even though we'd sworn off the idea of ever pastoring again or starting another church; we did start another one. Why? Because a woman, who had been with us from the beginning of our ministry and had remained a financial supporter for all those years, came to us with a word. She let us know that the building we had occupied in the beginning, back in 1977, was empty and available to us – for free. So, in December 1999, we started Gospel Outreach Church, and we were right back in the same building we had started in 22 years earlier. Our rose was blooming again, and in some very familiar soil.

The Gospel Outreach Church was awesome. I loved it! Many souls were saved, many families were coming and the church grew. Now, can you believe this? Darrell and Mary Anne Wilson, one of the couples who helped start the first church back in 1977, started this one with us too. Several people who had been with us before came back to help and be a part of what God was doing. Now that we were gonna pastor, we had to cut back on travel, and since the church was brand new and offered no hope of a salary, Clifton went to work for our son, Kelly, who was now a constructions superintendent.

This was a very good time in our lives. We were buying a great house and a ministry center combined. And I started teaching as a high school substitute. God is so very faithful. I didn't think I would ever be happy again after having to leave the best job of my life in Colorado, but those students loved me like they did at CBC, and I was so overwhelmed with blessings, I can't even begin to record them all here.

Even though it was a public school, I didn't hold back, not even once, when I had the opportunity to speak with a student about the Lord, or pray for them. Several of the teens, especially Cody's friends, came to our church and got saved. I was also able to minister to the teachers, and pray with many of them. I did this for four years and loved it with all my heart.

I jumped back in at the church, doing everything I could to make it a success. We got some of our old music team back together from the Lighthouse, and it was glorious. We had a simple ladies trio with guitar, but we sounded like angels. Later on, we added a keyboard and bass guitar. Clifton preached grace, and we had a heaven-on-earth experience there. It was a wonderful, healing time for me.

Our 'Plan' to Go Overseas

Dave and Bonnie Duell asked us to go to Portugal to minister in their place. They had overextended themselves with travel and they needed a fill-in, so we agreed to go with Dennis and Denise Capra and a team from the Capra's church.

There is a testimony of faith here. At the time, I didn't think the way we planned the trip was outstanding or out of the ordinary. Now, in hindsight, it seems like a great testimony.

We knew we had airline tickets, but we were "so broke we couldn't pay attention," as they say. We had scheduled a meeting in Blue Springs, Missouri with Tim Roofener, a meeting that had been scheduled before our overseas trip. Tim was a student of ours from the CBC days. He was one of Clifton's 'Timothy's' (Clifton actually had two ministers he mentored named Tim. The other was Tim Morris).

Tim's church was a small church, but we were believing that the love offering we would receive would be enough to cover the Portugal trip. As far as we knew, we would be paying all our hotel and food costs while we were in Portugal (even if we had known that most of that was being covered, a person still needs money for offerings, etc.)

At one point, I thought about the offering, and got a little panicked. We were counting on it to tide us over. Truthfully, we normally never gave the offering a second thought, and for many years we had forgotten about the offering, or the fact that we would actually be given money to do what we loved to do so much. Our hearts have always been for the people. We had received such powerful faith messages in the beginning of our ministry that we naturally trusted God, and had what some would call "foolishness for faith."

A few of you might agree that it was foolish of us to expect the money to come "on the way," especially overseas. I have to admit, I don't know many folks who would do it that way, but it had always worked for us in the past, so I figured God was faithful. After all, it was He who was sending us. Yes, the Portugal trip was HIS idea. To fill-in for the Duells was a huge honor for us, and we wanted to be used by God and make a good representation.

When we got to Tim's church, we were ready for the meeting, and gave it our all, as we always did. There were only a handful of people there that hot day in July. We had originally scheduled Tim's meeting for another date, but had moved it in order to be in Kansas City for the Portugal trip, which was coming up the following Tuesday. Tim's people had always loved us, and several had scheduled their vacations for after we were supposed to be there. When we switched, it meant they wouldn't be able to attend. We had no idea this had happened until after Tim told us.

That Sunday we ministered with power and anointing, as if there were a thousand people there. After the service, we went over to Tim's house to spend the night. We didn't say a word about money, or how we were believing to have a big offering. Tim brought a check in an envelope to our room. We said, "Thank you" and, as I remember, didn't open it right away. I had a migraine headache and Clifton was having pain in his face. I do remember Clifton said, (as a joke) in the midst of our moaning, "Well, God really knows how to bless us, huh?" That was a joke towards us, of course, because we never did blame God for anything. We were actually laughing at ourselves.

Later, I opened the envelope, and to our amazement it was a check for $1,500 dollars. That was such a blessing, and a testimony to God's faithfulness and His desire to always meet our needs and desires. We came out of the room, hugged Tim and thanked him, and he could tell we were surprised, so he told us they'd been collecting that offering ahead of time. (God knows what we need before we do!) Tim and Melissa are such gracious, generous souls, and they treated us like royalty while we were in their home. Their four children are mirrors of their parents' love for God, and a heart of servanthood has surely been transmitted to them.

When we arrived at the airport to fly out to Portugal, we were set with everything and feeling on top of the world. Then, a lady came rushing up to us with an envelope from Kansas City, and said she was so glad she had caught us. Someone had asked her to deliver the envelope, which had five 100 dollar bills in it! I don't know about you, but I saw God just enjoying Himself to the max, letting us know it is He who takes care of us, and that we never had to worry about finances.

Power in Portugal

The meetings in Portugal were hosted by Norton Da Silva and were electricity-filled with God's anointing and power to heal, set free, deliver, and save souls. They were some of the greatest meetings ever in our ministry! A woman had to wear special shoes because her feet weren't right – so we prayed, and she came back the next night with high heels on, dancing! The services were held on the top floor of a fire house where 500 people were crammed in, and it was rocking! The worship was heavenly. We sang a song that had "Na Na Na Na" in it (Waves of Mercy). Well, out of about a dozen nations represented there, that was a language we all understood, and we sang it loud and long, and greeted each other with a heavenly love. Every meeting was like that.

My reason for sharing this testimony about Portugal, the finances, and the outcome is to glorify God and to give you an example of how much He loves us and cares about every detail of our lives. I want to encourage you that if God has called you to do something, you are not on your own, you have the King of the Universe backing you up.

Sean Connery

Something funny happened in Portugal while we were there. At the time, Clifton had shaved his head. One evening, all of us were eating at this marvelous place, a restaurant on the ocean that served fresh seafood. Some of the men waiters were standing in the doorway pointing at Clifton and whispering. Then someone came and asked him if he was Sean Connery. I think he was signing autographs before we left. My husband, the movie star!

Chapter 10

Trials and Tribulations

The number ten means tribulation or trouble. I didn't plan for Chapter 10 to be about a very difficult time in our lives, but it has worked out that way.

Before we left Colorado, Clifton noticed a tingling feeling in his lips. He mentioned it to me, but neither of us thought much about it at the time. The sensation eventually turned into pain, and Clifton was finally in so much pain we sought medical help. To keep this part of the story short: we went to fifteen doctors and dentists before he could receive real help. We went to neurosurgeons, specialists in the dental field, had teeth pulled, and many other hopeful remedies, but all to no avail.

We were living in Indiana when we finally got a diagnosis. We discovered he had a condition called Trigeminal Neuralgia. The fifth cranial nerve was touching a blood vessel, causing intense, unbearable pain. Doctors call this the "suicide nerve." By the time we began treating the pain, Clifton was incapacitated, mostly because of medicine that never did actually help the pain. The pain meds kept him in a state of...let me see...how do I describe it? Zombie comes to mind.

He couldn't work, couldn't drive; he couldn't live a normal life. The church wasn't able to help much, and my small pay from the school didn't go very far. The medicine alone cost us over $50 every other day. Soon, we had to move to a smaller, cheaper house. I sure didn't want to do that.

It was a rough time in our marriage too. I actually said I wasn't going to move into the old farmhouse down the road, but Clifton wanted to go, so I gave in and off we went. The friend who owned the house had come to see us and said he needed someone in the house, and we agreed to buy it on contract from him. After getting moved in there, Clifton became incapacitated. Of course, we had people praying for us, and I prayed every day for my husband. That period of time is mostly a blur for me and the family. There were days when he couldn't even talk; all he could do was drag himself from the bed to the couch and from the couch back to the bed. Some days Clifton didn't even get dressed. We were trusting God as much as we knew how to, and He did provide for us day by day.

Soon, Clifton began forgetting to turn things off that he turned on, so he couldn't stay at home by himself. Our granddaughter, Emily, still talks about the time she came over to our house with her mother and the backyard looked like a lake. Clifton had left the outside water on after watering the dogs.

Deep In a Hole

We were going deeper into a hole every day. Some days, Clifton would have a good day. Our friends and family continued to pray – everyone we knew was praying for him.

Our church people stood with us, and allowed me to preach when he couldn't talk. The pain was so intense that Clifton actually couldn't speak. How is that for a demon attacking a preacher? I know you are waiting for the end of the story.

We were in a financial crunch, and we were raising a teenage boy, but God, who is rich in mercy (see Ephesians 2:4), came through for us in a tremendous way. We went about as normally as we possibly could, even accepting some evangelistic invitations. At times, Clifton could preach, and we always had awesome results in those meetings, just as if he was already healed. Also, I'd been planning a ministry trip overseas and our CCM partners had already paid for it. I had been invited to do a two week tour of preaching and teaching in churches in England and Ireland, doing ladies' meetings and other ministry opportunities. My friend, Anna Stewart, had spent two years setting all of it up, and I was very excited.

There were many dynamics working at that crucial time in our lives. I literally hated the house we were living in. I hadn't wanted to move there in the first place, but Clifton had been determined. The place had a new, 14-stall barn on three acres. Clifton soon saw the downside of the house itself and agreed with me that we needed to move.

Finally, Clifton told me to go and find something Cody and I liked, and he would move us all there. So, Cody and I made a list of what we wanted in a home. I trusted God every day to bring us through that time. I prayed constantly: I lived for Him, and sought guidance for every minute of every day. The

Holy Spirit spoke to me all the time and I listened and was obedient.

But God

Of course, we couldn't buy a house. We had no regular income and we had no money. We'd tried to apply for medical help and even disability, but we were told the list was long, and not to count on it. BUT GOD – when He's in the mix, all you need is faith. God was getting us in position to move: in a big way.

One day, when I went to the mailbox, I found a letter addressed to us with the return address of a church from a certain town in Missouri. We didn't know anyone from that town and I didn't open it right away. When I did open it later, the letter said that this church had a situation where their pastor had died suddenly. There was a short description of the church and the area, and they wanted us to pray for them, and help them find a pastor. Allen Speegle had sent them our name as someone who knew many people, and had contact with multiple pastors and church leaders. Allen felt we could help. We felt deep compassion for their situation, and we did pray about it.

Meanwhile, Clifton had planned a men's conference for that weekend. We had five pastors from five different states coming and bringing their men. Clifton was still so sick with his pain. It was only by faith he didn't cancel the meeting. He'd decided to take the letter from Missouri, and present it to those anointed men of God, feeling sure they would know someone who would and could do it.

Clifton had the letter in his pocket all weekend, but he said every time he would think of bringing it out, the Lord prompted him to leave it in his pocket. After the conference, Clifton told me that he felt compelled to keep the letter, and call them himself. Since we'd already planned an evangelistic trip out to Kansas City and then on to Douglass, Kansas, we made an appointment to meet with the board of the Missouri church on our way back home, which was to be on March 24, 2004.

Chapter 11

Beauty for Ashes

We left our home on March 19, 2004 to make the trip to Blue Springs, Kansas City and Douglass, Kansas. It was spring break for me and Cody, so he went with us. His birthday was March 17, and we had managed somehow to get him the guitar he wanted, which he brought on the trip. The night before we planned to leave, Clifton told me, "Geri, I can't go, I can't do this." He was in so much pain. I felt we were being compelled to go, and I believed the Holy Spirit was saying to "Go," so I offered to drive and let him rest. Clifton knew I could do the preaching or anything he needed, so he agreed to give it a try.

That morning, we were packed and ready to go. I felt I needed to leave our cell phone number with the neighbor, which we'd never done before, but the last time we'd been away from home, there'd been an issue with our dogs getting out of their pen, so I thought at least someone should have our number, in case they needed to call us. Kelly lived close by and was taking care of anything else we needed, so I taped our number to the neighbor's back door and off we went.

Clifton actually felt like driving, and he was having a good day. We did our church ministry in Blue Springs: Clifton preached an awesome message, and then we went on to Kansas City. We had time to talk between ourselves about the Missouri church, and the more we talked about it, the more we felt that it was something we wanted to do. Our hearts went out to the people there who'd lost their pastor, and the widow losing her husband made us cry out to God for them. Also, we felt our time at the Indiana church, now over five years, was almost up.

We hadn't discussed this with anyone. In Lynn Osborne's church, that Saturday night, a young man had a word for us, and began to speak things that pierced our hearts. He said the Lord had shown him a vision of Clifton and me standing on a great horizon, overlooking a harvest field, and he was hearing that we were about to enter a new place in our ministry. There was also a gigantic eye, God's eye, watching over us. It was a Wow word; a word, we felt, that answered what we'd been praying about. We received it, and later discussed the Missouri letter with the Osbornes, who immediately witnessed that the letter was a call from God.

So, Lynn and Shirley Osborne prayed over us, and we were off to the boondocks in Douglass, Kansas to do home meetings with some Catholic folks. There were a few couples and singles in the Bible study. Kenny and Lonia Turner were hosting the meetings, and we also were staying in their home. The anointing in those meetings was strong, and the people were ministered to and blessed in a great way. Several people were healed.

Everything Is Gone

The final night of those meetings was March 23. That morning we were abruptly woken up by our phone ringing and ringing. It was our neighbor. Her voice was frantic as she described the condition of our home, which she said was burning down. Everything was gone.

At first, I did not believe her, because her daughter-in-law had told me she was confused and had Alzheimer's. But in the end, she had it right. Our home was a pile of ashes. I was numb and in shock, grieving the loss of my family heirlooms. (My mother had just entrusted me with five generations of family heirlooms.) But God was getting ready to bless us abundantly. Our rose would bloom again.

We stayed in Kansas and finished the Bible study, even though we were in a state of shock. We were especially thankful that we had insisted that Cody come with us, and that we'd let him bring his new guitar. I'd streamlined our suitcases, since we were ministering in different places, so I'd only brought one church outfit.

We had one more night there. Of course, we were released by the couple hosting the meetings, but we knew we had the appointment the next day with the Missouri church, and besides, we had nothing to go back to. All our earthly possessions were gone. We preached Grace and God's love, which changed the lives of at least one Catholic couple, and several others who were there.

Restoration!

We began to receive phone calls, prayers and scriptures, especially about restoration, and the restoration began immediately. Job 42:10 says, *"The Lord gave Job twice as much as he had before."* Verse 11 says that his brothers and sisters and *"all that had been his acquaintance before,"* comforted him and gave him a piece of money, *"and everyone an earring of gold."* Well, we began to be abundantly blessed above measure, even before we got back home. Some ladies at the Bible study brought me jewelry and some new clothes. They also brought pillows and other nice things that night.

Our friends, Chuck and Johnna Smith, lived in a nearby town. I called her and she grabbed Chuck and met us for lunch and we had a party. Our good friends, Dave and Bonnie Duell, taught us to always have *"joy in temptation"* (James 1:2), which means to have a party when terrible things happen. One translation says, "Throw yourself a party." So we laughed, cried, ate Chinese food, and then Johnna took us shopping. She insisted. She and Chuck had talked it over, and that's what they wanted to do. Johnna purchased my entire wardrobe for England and for the rest of the winter. Clifton had a shopping cart loaded too. Johnna put me in a dressing room and brought me outfit after outfit.

So, the restoration began within hours of the house fire, and it continued, unabated, until we had more than we'd ever had before. Just like Job.

We started home the next day, stopping first at the Missouri church. We knew when we pulled into the parking lot that God was calling us there. Our two hour meeting went well. It took them some time to decide it was us God had chosen, but they finally did, and we moved to Missouri. Our first official service as their new pastors was May 2, 2004.

Hear the Spirit and Live

As a nugget of teaching and as a testimonial, I want to share here that it is vital to know the Holy Spirit, and His voice. As His children, we must learn how to hear Him. For example, natural circumstances would have kept us at home, but I knew we were to press forward and go on that trip. I usually go along with my husband's decisions on things (that's why we have been married all these years), but when I hear God more clearly than he does, I tell him, and Clifton has learned to listen. So guys, listen to your wives. When disastrous mistakes are made, it's a long, hard trip back up the mountain. If we had stayed home, a lot of people would have missed my husband's powerful anointing. If we had stayed home, the chances of all of us escaping that fire would've been slim.

The house fire started in the basement where a wire was stapled to the floor of our office. Those floors had been sanded, and Clifton had put many coats of heavy polyurethane on the hardwood to make them shine. That was like pouring gas onto a fire. Our bedrooms were upstairs; second floor. I thank God, every time this comes to my remembrance, that He led us out of the fiery furnace. God gave us *"beauty for ashes, the oil of joy for mourning, and the garment of praise for the spirit of heaviness."* (Isaiah 61:3) We had no insurance. The home owner had insurance on his house and property, but we hadn't bought any insurance for the contents inside the house.

More good news. When we arrived home, my passport and Clifton's approval for medical help were both waiting in our post office box. My overseas trip was still on and Clifton's healing was at hand.

Chapter 12

The Missouri Church

First of all, let me tell you, from the beginning in 2001, how we came to know about the Missouri church. This may help you to understand how important it is to follow God when you don't understand why He's leading you to do something; when He's directing you in a certain way that doesn't make sense to your natural mind. We can never go wrong when we're listening to God and being obedient, even though we don't understand at the time.

Our friends from St. Louis, Missouri, Steve and Gwen Corgan, had been to a series of meetings in Huntsville, Alabama. They sent us a set of tapes (yes, cassettes) from that meeting, and I was listening to them in my kitchen in Paoli, Indiana. At the end of one of the tapes, Janice Speegle, a lady from Eustis, Florida, announced she was having a Pastor's Wives Conference in Nashville, Tennessee in September 2001. My spirit leaped, like it had long ago, when I'd first heard the phrase, "Your Rose is Gonna Bloom Again."

I'd never gone anywhere to hear speakers when I didn't know the group who was doing the ministering, so I couldn't believe it myself when I started making plans to go. Janice had said, "Grab a couple of ladies and come to Nashville," so I did. I asked Marci Calloway and Roxanne Fealy if they would go, and they said yes. Even though I knew the Holy Spirit was leading me, I told the girls, "I know nothing about these people, so if it gets weird, we are outta there." I also told them, "Watch me. If I give the sign, we are gone."

Circles

Allow me to interject a little nugget here. There are many anointed, God-called ministries out there. Have you heard of "circles?" As humans, we tend to stay in one Christian "circle." I was that way. When I was a Baptist and in the Baptist circle, I thought we were the *only ones* that had it right. When I moved into the Faith circle I knew for sure, then, that we had all that was needed to make it in life. Then, on to the Grace circle, etc.

Over the years I've learned that nobody has it all. No circle or "camp" has all of God's revelation. We all have just a piece of the puzzle. Recently, I've moved into the prophetic circles and learned much from a good friend, Glenda Dowd-Tait, who God brought into my life supernaturally. Now I'm reading books that, at one time, I would've never touched. I've even stepped out in faith to invite speakers to my ladies' conferences that I knew were on a different page than I was, but I also knew their hearts, and that their love for God trumped anything they might say that wasn't exactly how I would say it.

One time, the Lord gave me an analogy of the intertwining of the Olympic circles. He said, "We overlap, yet we are still one." As a disclaimer, I must also say that there are some out there who are preaching heresy and gross error. For example, denying the validity of the Word of God. I keep my distance from those preachers, and pray that the revelation of the truth will once again bubble to the top of their minds (see 2 Timothy 2:24-25). A few of my friends are now saying that certain truths are not backed up by Scripture; they are friends who used to be in the same circle as me. It all boils down to listening to the Lord and following the Holy Spirit.

Anyway, I was going to the conference Janice Speegle was planning, because I knew God was leading me to go. The conference was planned for the weekend after 9/11. Of course, at that time, there were no flights available and Janice had to postpone the meeting until October. She called me and told me, and I told her there was only one weekend in October I could do it, so she planned her meeting for that weekend. (I thought that was just over the top, in a great way.) So, the three of us headed for Nashville at the appointed time and we were excited.

We had such a wonderful three days. Janice and I liked each other right away, and she invited us to Florida to a leadership conference they were having at their church. I talked Clifton into going, so then we got to meet Allen, Janice's husband. The leadership conference was awesome, we loved it. We saw them a few other times after that. Janice came to one of my ladies' conferences in Indiana and we got an opportunity to have lunch and fellowship together.

Allen had been friends with the pastor in Missouri who passed away in 2003 and he'd been helping that church by providing a pastor temporarily and had the word out for someone to go there and help that struggling church. Allen had given them our name, which is why Clifton had the letter in his pocket at the men's meeting.

An Open Door in 2004

In December of 2003, we were ministering in Colorado at Ed Shirley's church, Mountain High Christian Center, and Ed had a word for us that there would be an "Open Door in 2004." Again, my spirit soared inside me, because I knew there had to be some changes in our lives. For one thing, Clifton was desperately ill with the Trigeminal Neuralgia condition.

As we were being interviewed by the Missouri church board members, we knew we were supposed to be there. We believed God was calling us there. I had a tape in my purse that we'd done as a spontaneous team teaching at our Indiana church, and I left that with them. I had also compiled a biography about our ministry history, and when I got to the end, I was going to write about Clifton's illness, but God spoke to "Stop there," and not write it down. I knew He said that, so I figured He had a plan.

The home the church provided for us was perfect. It was a two-story house with dormers, like the one Clifton had built for me in Indiana. The inside was just beautiful, and I was in a daze at the porches, the lake in the back, the surrounding woods; it was all very much like our place in Indiana we'd sold to Kelly and Darlene while we were in Colorado. I knew from the day I saw it (the day after the interview), that I would be sitting there at the lake, praying and sitting on the back deck, writing down my thoughts and preparing my messages. It seemed like a piece of "Heaven on Earth" to me. Clifton liked it, too, and was happy that I was happy.

Good Times

Clifton and I were both ecstatic to have such a sweet group of people to love and pastor; to teach the Word of God to. The church building was very nice, and it had everything we'd ever had a vision for, right down to the gymnasium. We saw "room for people." We planned to be there from then on – till Jesus came to get us.

Even though we had no insurance when our home burned, the people we'd ministered to over the years came through and helped us tremendously, just like the scripture from Job. One man, our ministry partner Dave, who we'd helped and loved when he needed it, heard about our home burning down, and actually offered to build us a house on his property. He said we could live there till we died.

By that time, we'd been accepted as the new pastors at the Missouri church, and Clifton told Dave we had a home to move to. Dave said, "Geri is gonna need furniture," so he bought us a houseful of furniture by opening a line of credit at a furniture store in town. Now I ask you, who has had that happen? Not me, that's for sure. Not until then! God meant it when He said he would restore "more than before." God's Word comes true and He keeps His promises. He blesses us back abundantly when we sow, and by then, Clifton and I had sown into thousands of lives.

We were able to buy a good car, a navy blue Lincoln Town Car, to replace our Cadillac, which had over 200,000 miles on it. It took all the money we had left at that time: we put several thousand dollars down, and still had a payment for three years. It was going to feel good to have a nice looking, dependable car to pull up to that nice church. Smile.

We Accepted the Offer

We didn't know yet what the church was going to pay us: it wasn't even brought up until May 2, the day the board met with us and made their "offer." Clifton and I had already decided God was sending us to Missouri, and that the salary wasn't an issue with us. We knew from past experience that God always knows what He's doing. We knew how to live on nothing: we'd raised three kids on nothing except what people sowed into us out of their love for us, and their obedience to God. (Clifton did work construction again for a brief period before Cody was born, but we'd always lived by faith.)

The "offer" was a house to live in and a small weekly salary. My heart sank a little, but we weren't moved. We knew God would take care of things. Health insurance was also offered, and eventually we did have that.

So, we jumped right in at the Missouri church. We were used to working hard, and we did. We told the board we weren't going to come in and change everything, but that there would be some slow changes and our goal was to make the church as good as it could be. To win souls – that was our heartbeat. They were all in agreement, so we thought that was what they wanted too.

Soon, Clifton added more services and we began to grow. Some Sundays there was standing room only. There was a need to build a second-phase onto the church to make room for all the growth. The architectural plans were in the pastor's office, so we thought everyone would be thrilled that his (the deceased pastor) plan was going forward.

I also need to interject here that Clifton was able to have a medical procedure called "Gamma Knife" surgery on his head to relieve the Trigeminal Neuralgia pain, and after the surgery, he was a new man, with a new lease on life. What a miracle! Gamma Knife surgery is a procedure where a "helmet," which looks like a colander (metal and full of holes), is placed on the patient's head and secured with screws into the skull. A ray of radiation is focused through the right hole of the helmet, causing a scarring of the nerve, which gives the aggravated blood vessel a cushion, so to speak, and thus the blood vessel isn't touching the nerve and the pain is alleviated.

School Days

We opened a School of Ministry – a Bible college – and 30 students signed up. We were all so happy. Clifton was teaching them grace. I covered subject matter pertaining to everyday living in the victory that has already been provided for us. The course was entitled "Victorious Christian Living," and was based on Joel Osteen's book, "Your Best Life Now." We had a teacher come in and present "Biblical Finances," a video series by Robert Morris. That teaching was excellent. It changed our lives financially. (I heartily recommend Morris's book, "The Blessed Life.")

We have been generous givers and tithers all our Christian lives, but Robert Morris' course went beyond our giving to the church, and taught us how to have personal money for emergencies instead of always needing a miracle. We also gleaned much from Andrew Wommack's material, "Blessings and Miracles" and the "Excel" Bible school curriculum put together by Denise Capra, which includes teachings from multiple, anointed men and women of God.

More Miracles

I taught a course on prayer, and we tried to cover all the subject matter pertaining to life and godliness (see 2 Peter 1:3). A number of students graduated from our School of Ministry. Our rose was blooming again, and we felt we were fulfilling our vision and the vision of the church.

We took a team of students to Ireland and saw many miracles. We went into the streets, we held meetings in a Methodist church basement, we saw souls saved, and many received a revelation of grace. Men and women literally came in from the streets when they heard our music. During a Sunday morning meeting, a woman named Grace came forward for prayer for a lump in her breast, which completely disappeared during the service!

Another woman had had an accident 25 years earlier, which caused a deformity in her leg so that she wasn't able to walk without severe pain and a limp. Her leg was healed during one of the evangelistic meetings and that caused no small stir! Our entire trip was like that. Clifton and I took a train to Dublin and preached in a church pastored by friends I'd met in 2004, Paddy and Pauline Keegan. It was glorious, and our team saw the gospel being put into action.

During our two and a half years at the Missouri church, we brought in all our highly gifted friends from across the U.S. and around the world to preach to our people. We loved our folks so much, and we wanted to expose them to the most powerful and anointed preachers we knew. I can honestly say, from my heart, that we had a pure motive in advancing that church.

Show Me

You may have heard that Missouri is called the "Show Me" state. Now we know why. Trust is not a common factor to this area. When Clifton, Cody and I moved to this town in Missouri, we didn't know one single person – not one – but we'd heard the call from God and we considered the move a new beginning. Prophetic words had also come to us many times over the years (and from many friends), saying that the message we brought was needed in Missouri – a revelation of the unconditional love of God. (Good teaching about the grace and unconditional love of God is needed everywhere.)

Something else we did at the Missouri church was to begin a Thursday night "Power Team" training where we taught the practical ministry of laying on of hands for healing (Mark 16:15-18). After we trained them, our students were sent out to the community to do the stuff. This brought many new folks into the church.

One example was a six-month-old baby we'd heard about who was in the hospital, in a coma. One of our teams went and laid hands on that baby, prayed for her healing, and she came out of the coma and went home the next day! Let me tell you, that caused a chain effect of salvations. About thirty people were added to the church.

Catering to a 'Lower Class'

Many of the new folks came with tattoos, with handkerchiefs on their heads; not looking like traditional church goers at all. Our response was "Praise the Lord!" However, it is sad to say, that certainly wasn't the reaction of everyone at the church. One complaint we heard was, "It seems we're catering to a lower class of sinners now."

We put together a tent meeting, using our gospel tent on the church's property, and one of the new converts, the grandpa of the baby healed in the hospital, was healed of cancer and received the baptism of the Holy Spirit! Many folks were filled with the Holy Spirit during those meetings, and many were added to the church. Lives were changed forever.

While doing Bible studies at the local rehab center, we got permission to bus the patients to church on Sunday mornings. Those folks were getting delivered, saved, and ministered to in such a powerful way that they went back and got more and more of their friends to come. For two years in a row there were nearly 300 saved per year.

Their stay at the rehab center was for only 30 days, so those folks were coming and going constantly, but the results were phenomenal. Clifton would say at the beginning of the service, "How many have come to get saved today?" Hands went up all over the house. To say we were ecstatic doesn't even begin to describe our excitement!

One of the rehab doctors came to see what was going on. He wanted to know the reason his patients were all doing so well and why they were talking about our church all the time. The day he came to visit, there were extra chairs brought in and the house was packed. The doctor met with us for lunch after the service and said he wanted to be a part of the church. So he and his wife started coming, and they also became involved with the Bible school.

Trouble Starts to Brew

Speaking of the visitors from the rehab center, a former member of the church's leadership made the comment that "those people" were leaving their cigarette butts on church grounds. That comment was made in our weekly Monday morning meetings where we normally discussed the service the day before. There were other things going on behind the scenes (criticism from those holding the power card), which we were beginning to hear about, but we believed the anointing and the success of the church would win out. We tried to let those attitudes and criticisms roll off us.

The problem was the owner of the church (yes, the owner), his wife, and the former pastor's wife were the only three legal church board members. The owner attended the church very rarely, just a few times a year, so he was getting his (false) information from somewhere inside the body. Also, it was a "family church," a fact we didn't know in the beginning. The church leadership was comprised mostly of family members.

When we first began at the church, we didn't change the leadership of any of the departments, but instead met with each one to hear their hearts, because those leaders had been successful in their ministry to the children and young people. The former pastor's mother loved us, but she couldn't accept that we were taking her son's place. Later on, that caused much grief for her and us.

So, even though we were giving it our all and seeing great results, there was constant pressure, debate and criticism coming from the former leadership. Our rose had bloomed brightly for a season, but soon it would face a very severe Missouri winter.

Chapter 13

Trouble in Paradise

In the beginning, Clifton had made it very clear that there was one non-negotiable factor in us accepting the pastorate at the Missouri church. He was asked in the first meeting, when we were still talking about our coming there to pastor, "Is there a non-negotiable?" Yes, Clifton said, he would have to be in charge. They agreed, as they had been used to a pastor-led church, and that's also what we knew how to do.

Big Problems

The only problem was, someone else was in charge – behind the scenes – only, we didn't know it. So you can imagine our struggle.

That issue started right from the beginning, and within thirty days, we knew we had big problems. We had no idea when we accepted the pastorate, that there would be a power struggle. We went there believing that the church wanted a pastor, and the people (the church body) did. But it became evident that the former leadership just didn't want to let go of control of the church.

I tried to see things from their perspective, but there was great stress with that situation. They thought we were trying to take the church away from them. However, we'd learned a long time ago how to press through obstacles, so that's what we did: we stayed and did what we were called to do – pastor that church as best we could. We prayed and sought the Lord on what to do. Remember, we had left our children and grandchildren in Indiana, plus my mother and all our other family. We had made a big commitment by coming to Missouri, so in our hearts, we were there to stay.

Too Much Salvation

When the big day came in July 2006, a special board meeting was called. We weren't sure what it was all about, but Clifton said, "They're going to ask us to leave." I thought he was crazy. I didn't believe it, but, alas, it was true.

At the meeting, a resignation paper was brought out and we were asked to sign it. Clifton said he wouldn't. We were offered $50,000 to go away. We didn't actually see the paper because one of the board members grabbed it, ripped it up, and threw it on the floor. The owner's wife said to us, "Well that just cost you $50,000."

But God hadn't released us, so we couldn't leave. Only two people in that meeting knew what was really happening. The others were either men we had chosen to be on the board, or original members who we left on because they seemed supportive of all we had been accomplishing. Sadly, only two members present at that meeting were legally on the church's Missouri State incorporation papers, and that ruled.

I asked, "What is your grievance?"

They answered, "You preach too much salvation."

The "powers that be" had the authority. Three people. Three – out of a church full of others who loved us, our ministry, and wanted us to stay. Clifton told the "church owner" that if he was going to leave, he would have to get up in front of the church on Sunday morning and announce it to the people. He refused.

Since then, we learned in a church leadership conference put on by Allen and Janice Speegle that most pastors leave their churches because of the negative influence of just three to five people. We wouldn't have left because of those three, but we had no choice. They legally ran the church.

I think it shows more integrity, on my part, to just speak briefly about our departure, rather than rehearse all the injustices. However, I do want to say this right now: we never even saw the finances and we were not in charge of any money except the "Love Account," which was set aside for charitable giving to the needy.

We were paid about half of what it took for us to live each month. In the beginning, there were no benefits for us. We didn't know, until near the end, about the "financials" of the church. We were only invited to one finance meeting. It was shocking, especially since I'd been told there was no money to reimburse me for the things I bought for the office, or for anything else. We paid for our own gas for ministry, oil changes. Everything.

Before the End

One time we received a check from Indiana for several thousand dollars. It had been owed to us from many years ago, and showed up right on time. We had to depend on outside finances to live when we pastored that church. We did evangelistic meetings, and received support from our Clifton Coulter Ministry outreaches and partners.

During our two and a half years at the Missouri church, Clifton and I tried to move forward in the face of debilitating circumstances and a wall of jealousy that caused me much stress. My hair came out; I had (for the only time in my life) high blood pressure and had to be treated for it. I had migraines and many Saturday nights I couldn't even close my eyes because of the stress of facing the Sunday morning service.

The music was another grief. I'd led our worship in Indiana for seventeen years, then for five more years when we came back from Colorado. During all that ministry, we'd never had any problems that weren't ironed out immediately. I had a philosophy: if someone or something got "crossways," we didn't move one inch till it was prayed through and settled. There seemed to be unrest and unhappiness among the worship team. They did not honor me as the leader. Someone was always upset about something. On one major holiday, the whole team except for my sweet keyboardist, Jan, just did not show up. Somehow we pulled off the worship between us.

The Power of Unity

Our praise and worship team had a very special dynamic during the Lighthouse days. We were in unity (Psalms 133:1) and we sounded so good, the producer of our worship recording called us "an orchestra." I truly didn't know how blessed we were. That group really flowed with each other, we loved each other, and we didn't have anyone wanting to be in the limelight.

Another thing was, everyone understood the line of authority. I was the leader and yet I never had to say, "Hey, I'm the leader." I took all of that for granted, and learned, later on, that our team was very special. The devil hates it when God's people flow in unity and have an anointing. He doesn't stop with his harassment. That's why we, as the body of Christ, continually need new beginnings.

We Have to Leave

Before the end, we ran into Allen Speegle at a conference in Tennessee, and told him of our dilemma. He felt somewhat responsible for us being there (we never felt he deserved any blame at all), and he wanted to help. He was actually called by the Missouri church to come and help them, so he knew what we'd been through, and he said he was, "100% in our corner."

Allen had visited the Missouri Church about a year before the end and had made some changes. He tried to be neutral and fair. All were in agreement, but the changes lasted less than a year, when they held the big meeting and asked us to leave.

When I went to bed the night after we were told to leave, I felt a peace and a relief like a thousand pound weight had been lifted off my chest. Clifton felt the same way. Then, at 3 a.m., we received a phone call. The president of the church corporation, the head board member who had fired us, asked to meet with Clifton, so Clifton went to the Huddle House in the middle of the night. They drank coffee and talked till daybreak.

The man said he'd made a big mistake and wanted us to stay. Clifton insisted that they go back to the original agreement: that we would be able to direct the church without any outside pressure. Clifton also wanted the directors changed on the state incorporation papers. Though it was agreed upon by both men, it never happened. A month later, we were told by the head board member and his wife that they weren't sticking to their agreement, so we resigned.

Before things changed, our beautiful navy blue Lincoln had been traded by the owner of the church for a brand new Lincoln. Our own car was very nice and we were satisfied with it, but we didn't reject the gift. The keys to the new car were handed to Clifton and he was told, "This is your car." It had been put in the church's name for tax purposes. A pay raise and some benefits had also developed as the church grew.

Stripped of Everything

Once we resigned, we were stripped of everything in one day. No car, no home, no salary, no severance pay. Nothing. They actually sent a tow truck after the car. We'd already had it detailed, done an oil change, and filled it with gas.

Everything we had in our possession that belonged to the church was placed inside the car and delivered to the attorney as we'd been instructed to do. We also had been told we could stay in the parsonage until January, but instead we received an eviction notice in late September, and had to hurriedly find a new place to live.

Still, God didn't release us from Missouri. Personally, I wanted to go home, but Clifton was strong and said we weren't going to run out. He said we would, "Jump out in front and act like it was a parade."

The Sunday we left, some of the church people had called, and come by our home. They wanted us to be their pastor. So, the following Wednesday night, we rented a room in the back of a restaurant in town, and we had church. A new adventure was about to begin.

Could our crushed rose come back to life?

Chapter 14

Grace Family Outreach Church

On a hot, humid Wednesday night, in the back room of a restaurant in Park Hills, Missouri, on August 16, 2006, we started our new church. It was absolutely wonderful! By the way, remember God's numbers? The number eight is new beginnings: August 16, 2006 = August is the eighth month, the 16th is two more eights, and 2006 added together equals eight. All new beginnings. Of course, this number "coincidence" wasn't planned, and I didn't' see it for some time. But when I did, I was ecstatic. God knows what He's doing, whether we do or not.

We were free. No more having a feeling of someone questioning everything we did, and everything we wanted to do. We started with a great group of people: the cream of the crop, we thought. We found a temporary rental home in the country. We were able to buy another Lincoln. We continued with the same salary and benefits we had worked up to, and never missed a week. Actually, for the first time in our ministry, we were blessed with enough money to not struggle.

Our Rose Blooms

When we left the Missouri church, one of my tape albums was on the desk, and God guided my eyes to the title, "Your Rose Will Bloom Again" (believe it or not). The new church building that opened up for us had a large beautiful rose blooming out in front, and that was my sign!

Our new church did, through a series of circumstances, end up in that building, and we were there for two years. The building was for sale. Our people thought we could buy it, so we started the process with a local banker who had the authority over the building, which was in repossession from another church group. The bank that actually owned the building was in St. Louis. We cleaned that building (which hadn't been cleaned for a very long time, it was gross), from foyer to bathrooms. We scrubbed with toothbrushes and soon had it standing tall.

Our vision and goal has always been, to win souls and to teach and disciple believers in the unconditional love of God. Grace. The gospel message is one of Grace. God loves us no matter what we do, where we are, where we have been, or even what we will do as we continue to live our lives. Our sins were paid for – past, present, and future – when Jesus hung on the cross for sin itself (see Colossians 2:13). The Apostle Paul greeted his followers in all his letters with grace and peace, and then signed them, "The grace of our Lord Jesus Christ be with you all."

The Freedom Message

This message is liberating, it is the freedom message. It is the message Jesus taught Paul, and He gave Paul the mandate to preach it to the Gentiles. This Gospel of Grace is a powerful truth that changes lives – it sure changed mine and Clifton's.

The enemy of our souls hates this message because it sets people free to serve the Lord with no condemnation. Satan loves to lie to the saints of God and tell them they aren't good enough to speak the name of Jesus, and that they certainly haven't measured up to God's standards well enough to testify of His goodness and blessing to them. But the truth is: when we believe on Jesus, we become holy, sanctified, and blameless in the sight of God forever (see Ephesians 1:4).

The devil has no claim on you after you receive Jesus. You are free. Jesus did it all on Calvary. It's a done deal. He paid for your sin, your sickness, your guilt, your shame and nailed it to His cross, once-for-all. Colossians 2:10 says that we are *"complete in Him."* Complete means lacking nothing. We are not in need of anything. Jesus paid it all, and provided everything for us. The Bible says, *"If God gave His only Son for us, how much more will He freely give us all things?"* (Romans 8:32)

The teaching of God's unconditional love is the message people need to hear. There are precious saints of God thinking God is mad at them, when the Bible says that all of Gods' wrath was appeased when Jesus hung on the cross. All of God's "against-ness" towards us was washed away at the cross. There really is "Power in the Blood" of Jesus!

We finally "got it" that the devil hates this truth of God's word so much that he continually tries to get the preachers who teach it to STOP. We believe that is the reason we've been so vehemently attacked over the years.

First Anniversary

After a while, our church was growing, we were winning souls, and teaching students in our own School of Ministry. I was producing radio broadcasts every week. We were enjoying life. We celebrated our one year anniversary in August 2007, and had some glorious meetings.

Friends from all across the United States came and helped us celebrate. It was simply awesome for us and for our church people. Charlie and Jill LeBlanc came the last day. We had a packed house and an anointed time of worship and celebration. Then, Charlie had a word for the church. He said, "You are getting ready to turn a corner. God has seen your faithfulness, and He is moving in this church, and there are new beginnings right around the corner." We received that prophetic word and the church was electrified with the anointing that day! It was a great time.

Just for the record, our people here in Missouri are more precious than gold. Why would we still be here if that wasn't true? Our family is all in Indiana.

Chapter 15

Ivan

This chapter has been very difficult to write, but it is an important part of my story.

Ivan is Clifton's middle brother. Clifton is the youngest of five (technically six), children. The eldest Coulter brother is Phillip. There was a still-born brother after the firstborn daughter, but in the days of home births and stillborns, names were not given. His mother told me the baby weighed nine pounds. It was a breech birth, and back then it was difficult to save a baby in that situation. Heartbreaking for the parents. Clifton and Ivan were four years apart, but were close to each other as they grew up. As an adult, Ivan distanced himself from his family, and we only saw him periodically; the last time was in 1995, when he moved us to Colorado.

In 2002, Ivan was sent to prison for an accident he had in his 18-wheeler. From the look of Ivan's arrest photo, there appeared to be a facial drawing on one side, so we believed he actually had a stroke. All indications from the police report pointed to stroke symptoms. However, for whatever reason, that evidence was never presented in court.

At the scene of the accident, Ivan was immediately sent to jail, instead of to a hospital. He had run from the police, driving northward on a southbound Interstate highway in South Carolina and caused seventeen accidents. Thank God no one was hurt – miracle of miracles. Ivan said he thought someone was trying to kill him. His mind wasn't right, which was also an indication that he was sick.

Ivan Makes a Big Change

Ivan spent five years in prison and substance abuse rehab, and while there, he was born again (see John 3:3). He began a process of trying to restore himself back to his three daughters, who he'd abandoned 25 years earlier, but whom he still loved with all his heart and soul. He tried to reach out to all his family members.

Unfortunately, Ivan had destroyed all his relationships over the years through drug and alcohol abuse. Even Clifton was only led one time to go to prison for a visit, and that was with his cousin, Brack. However, the Word of God went into action. The mother of Ivan's children, Charlesetta, was a great Christian woman while she was married to Ivan and raising their girls (and still is to this day). She taught Ivan's daughters to pray for their Daddy. The girls all grew up to be awesome women of God. While they loved their dad, they'd been accustomed to his erratic behavior when he would visit them. They were appalled by it, and had to limit his visits to their homes. Ivan's problem was that he was an alcoholic. That led to some extreme behavior he deeply regretted later.

One of the things Ivan wanted to do was help younger men change their lives and not leave their families. Those actions, in his own life, had led to guilt he'd endured for years. He knew God had forgiven him, but he found it difficult to forgive himself, and he constantly needed reminding that the past was the past. All he could do was go forward now, and make up for lost time, which was what he was trying to do. He had big plans.

When Ivan was released from prison, he had nowhere to go. He had written us a letter and asked if he could come stay at our house. We had three of Kelly's boys and their mother, Darlene, living with us, and Cody too, so every room was full. Darlene wanted to get her own place though, and she had a job, so she went and found a house, and they moved out soon after Christmas.

A New Guest

From the minute he arrived at our home, I could tell Ivan was different and for the entire time Ivan was with us, we never once had a cross word. In fact, to the contrary, Ivan was over-the-top nice: respectful, courteous and appreciative. The perfect gentleman.

Ivan loved going to church. We were in the middle of our School of Ministry Bible College: teaching three hours on Sunday afternoon, two hours on Monday nights, and regular church on Wednesdays, but that still wasn't enough for Ivan. He wanted to go to church every night. What a tremendous blessing he was.

Clifton was overjoyed that their childhood relationship had been restored. They rode horses, and Clifton was able to spend time with Ivan. We were helping him get a new life going, and then Clifton would get back to pastoring the church (Clifton had taken a break to spend time with his brother.)

In January, we had Dave Duell visit the church, and Ivan received a touch from God like he'd never experienced before. We had shared a lot about the goodness of God, and Ivan was learning that God's love is unconditional. We also talked about 2008 being a year of New Beginnings. Our slogan was "Life is Great in 2008."

Reconciliation

Ivan was already experiencing many of those new beginnings, especially the reconciliation between himself, his daughters, and his grandchildren. On their way back from South Carolina, Clifton and Ivan had stopped over in Kentucky to see everyone. Then, Phylissa and her son T.J. came at Christmas time for a visit. Ivan was crazy about his grandson, T.J. They made plans to go fishing, and Ivan gave T.J. a pup.

Ivan had a pair of glasses coming, so he could get his driver's license. He was given a pickup truck, and had two job offers. Life was good for all of us. We were trying to find a different house so we could all live better. Renting was okay, and had served its purpose, but now we needed our own place. (The farmhouse was supposed to be only temporary, because we'd been forced to find something quickly due to the situation at the church.) Ivan signed up for Social Security, and didn't think he would qualify, but he did, and received his first check in January. He was so excited! He wanted to help with the house payments.

In December, we traveled to Kansas City and Ivan had stayed behind at the house, taking care of our animals and watching over things. January is the time we always go to Florida to rest and plan our upcoming ministry year. The previous year had been one of many trials and stress. I was done in, kaput, and I felt like I couldn't make one more decision. I told Clifton, "Don't ask me any questions, don't have me make a single decision. I have to totally rest my head. I feel like my brain is mashed potatoes." Kelly's wife, Darlene, and three of their four boys had lived with us for eight months after Kelly left them with us. That too, was a stressful time, but also one of investing into those boys and being there for their healing and restoration.

God, How Could This Happen?

Darlene and the boys had found a home and moved out just two weeks before we left on our Florida trip. We had some friends, Ken and Ellen Gerry from Indiana, meeting us down there. They're easy to be around, and wouldn't demand anything from us, so we were excited to get there and catch up with them, and knew we would have a great time. We picked them up at the airport on the evening of January 19.

Early Sunday morning on January 20, we received a phone call from home. Our house was burning up, they said, and Ivan was dead. The fire had started in the attic of our family room, caused by faulty wiring.

Our beloved pets: Rhoda, a Rat Terrier and Charlie Cat, Cody's cat, were inside. Bubba, a yellow Lab, and our Molly Kitty, who'd wisely demanded to be an outside cat when we moved into the farmhouse, were both safe.

The house was declared a total loss by the insurance adjuster. Our rose seemed to disappear – buried somewhere in the ashes.

So many questions! Oh God! If "Life was Great in 2008," had I missed something? God, how could this happen? Life was NOT great.

Chapter 16

New Beginnings

Chapter 16. Sixteen is two eights. As you know by now, eight is God's number for new beginnings. For example, there are seven days in a week and then the eighth day is a new beginning. There are seven steps from the outer court and then the eighth step goes into the Holy of Holies, where a new beginning has been appropriated: we stand in the presence of God. There are many more examples of the number eight being the number for new beginnings.

God spoke to me that Ivan got a new beginning unlike any other. He had begun his new life with Jesus in eternity. Before we had left home that January morning, Ivan had looked at me and said, with a smile, "Geri, this is going to be a good year."

Numb

As for Clifton and me, we didn't feel like we had a new beginning. We felt whipped. Numb. We didn't know if we could continue. We packed, got plane reservations to leave Florida, and so did the Gerry's. We left the day after we arrived, with no vacation, and now all the stress. God spoke to

Clifton that this was an attack to get him to quit preaching. If Clifton had said, "Let's quit," I would've responded, "Okay!"

That was Sunday, but we'd already invited friends from Tampa, Jimmy and Zoe White, down to visit and have lunch. I'd purchased a lot of groceries for the week, so I went ahead and fixed a ham, with all the trimmings, and a dessert, and we didn't tell them the tragic news until they arrived. I think back on that now as I write this, and I don't know how I did all that. I remember feeling like it wasn't true. How could this be? I thought.

Actually, I think we all left on Monday.

Ivan would tell his daughters and other family members on the phone (I often overheard him say), "Clifton is the best preacher in the world, and so is Geri." What a restoration that was. Ivan and I didn't always see eye to eye during his former life. Smile. (That's a kind way to say it.) When he was trying to come live with us, Ivan made some big promises, and I was skeptical, but he held up his end perfectly and went beyond his own words.

In the Cleft of the Rock

When Jennifer, a lady in our church, heard the news, she went immediately to Deb, another friend in church, and asked if she could stay with her and let us have her apartment. That was an unspeakable blessing and a wonderful gift; deeper and wider than we could've known.

We were able to go to Jennifer's place and be alone. All we wanted to do was hear from God, make some plans, and receive healing. There was no TV. We went about doing what had to be done, and waited on the Spirit of God for direction. I felt I was in the "cleft of the rock." During that time, I wrote an article for the Faith Ministries Magazine about our loss, and the new beginning.

Ivan and Clifton had been looking for a house for us to buy. Clifton and I had gone to the bank in November and been pre-approved for a loan. We'd found a house we thought we were going to be able to buy. We had bid on it in January and we were told then that we were the only bidders. It looked like it was ours. It seemed to be "perfect" and we were to hear for sure while we were on our trip to Florida. After the devastating news, we felt somewhat relieved that at least we were going to have a place to go – a house to live in and call our own. But the day after we returned from our (almost) trip, we received the phone call that someone else had bid a little higher, and we weren't going to get the house.

Let me interject a little lesson here: I was beyond sad. I cried till there were no more tears. I was so disappointed. Whatever wind that might have been left in me was knocked completely out of my sails. I felt shot; completely defeated.

God Has a Better Plan

But God had a better plan. This is my lesson: Trust God! Know, for sure, that He does keep your best interest right in the middle of His heart, and He will pull you through and make things better. "Isn't that hard to do, Sister Coulter?" you might ask. YES, it is. But where else could I turn? I have felt, at times, that I simply couldn't continue with life, but I have to say that God has always had a plan for me, even when I felt like I was at the very bottom (or under the bottom) of the barrel, as they say.

To sum up this story, we received contents insurance on our belongings in the house. Our policy was small, compared to what we lost. Materially, we received about 25% of the value of our things. My mother was insistent that we get renters insurance after the Indiana fire. Thank God for Mom. I wouldn't have done it if she hadn't pushed me.

Because of the way the insurance policy was worded, we got nothing for Ivan's death. If he'd been a visitor, there would have been $100,000 worth of coverage included in that policy. But there was nothing for family members. The owner of the home received a tremendous amount of money for his loss, but we never even got so much as a phone call from him. What is the matter with people? His daughter and son-in-law looked after the house for him, collected the rent, and fixed things, etc. They told us they were sorry.

It was very upsetting to us that Ivan's life was counted as a casualty that deserved nothing. Very difficult. Clifton wanted Ivan's girls to have an inheritance. Ivan wanted them to have something as well, and he had been working towards making it up to them for all the years he hadn't been around. Ivan talked about his girls constantly, and was very proud of them. He also talked to our son, Kelly, and told him not to leave his family – that he would regret it someday.

A New Home

Most of the contents insurance money was used as a down payment on a new place to live. It was the house that Ivan and Clifton had picked out earlier. I didn't agree to it when they initially told me about it. In December, I'd driven out there and said it was too close to the road for our dogs.

After the fire, though, it seemed to be the "God appointed" home for us. It was a piece of property with eight acres (actually, I found out when we received our property tax bill that it was 8.8 acres), two barns, and a place for a swimming pool. We received finances from so many people loving on us and helping us that we were able to furnish our home and buy mowers, a tractor, and everything we needed. There was a spring-fed stream running through the property that always provided the horses with fresh water. We were very excited to own our own home again.

The bedroom furniture and some other things weren't burned. They were smoke damaged though, and everyone said that smell would never come out. The furniture was expensive: provided by a ministry partner of ours who'd set up a credit line for me to replace the contents we lost in the first fire. You're thinking, "Wow!" I know!

We moved the bedroom furniture out of the house, cleaned it, and put it in our new place. Miraculously, it was impossible to detect that it had ever been through a fire. The "smoke smell" miracle included some kitchen chairs and a table given to me by Ellen Gerry, and a few other things.

Finally, we were starting to settle in. We began to realize what had actually happened to us and we began to miss our beloved "Rhoda" doggie who had been in Ivan's bed the night of the fire. She died from smoke inhalation. Clifton and I were in such a state of grief.

Slowly though, we started feeling better, and began getting excited again about the church. We continued to preach and serve, and just be there. In spite of our grief, the church continued to grow, and there were souls saved every week and even during the week – every day. Lives were being changed for eternity. It was exciting, and we were experiencing some degree of healing. The church had a wonderful shower for us for our new home. We felt loved, and we loved them. Our rose felt like it was opening up again!

Then, the enemy launched an attack, and it was the most shattering thing that had ever happened to us.

Chapter 17

Betrayal

In April 2008, it was beginning to settle in on us what had happened in January. We were devastated, but simultaneously coming to a revelation of God's great plans for us and the church. We simply loved our new home, and we felt peace there. Healing was coming, washing over us. For me personally I felt my home was a reward, a "compensation" for all we'd been through. For the first time in our lives I had the finances (due to some generous gifts from friends) to furnish my home and decorate it the way I wanted to. We also had some insurance money that we'd put back to finish the basement.

Red Walls

I was having the time of my life. I had plans for each room, and had already started with the kitchen. Red. Yes, against my husband's better judgment, I went with red. Well, one red wall, and then Clifton liked it so well, he painted another one red. I'd planned to go back through the house and decorate each room. All the walls had been painted off-white. I was having the time of my life.

I will never forget a Tuesday around the third week of April. Deb and Ruth came by to see the house, and to take me to Applebee's for lunch. No real occasion – they just loved me and wanted to come see my home and what all I'd done to it. Before we left for lunch, we sat on the front porch in my new, white wicker furniture and drank ice tea. We had such a wonderful time. They were truly excited for me and Clifton, and for the blessings we were receiving. At Applebee's, we talked and laughed, and had a fun time.

I drove away in my Mustang convertible, thinking back to when I had no car, and the times I had to carry water and oil in my trunk because I never knew if I'd make it where I needed to go. I reflected on our lives, and the hard times, but then I thought more about the way God had restored us and given us new beginnings. I was thanking Him for all His wonderful blessings. I was feeling good again. I was being delivered from grief.

The Phone Call

Then I got the phone call.

It was Clifton and his voice was almost frantic; not like him at all. He'd been working on our new church building, and he said, "Geri, you have got to get up here, right now! There's an uprising in the church."

I couldn't imagine what could be wrong. We'd been having the most wonderful services. Since the fire Clifton had a new, fresh anointing – it was the most powerful anointing I'd seen in years.

Our attendance was up over a hundred people on Sundays, with new people coming every week, and there had been six souls saved in church the week before all the confusion began. We had a new worship team, an anointed, wonderful couple and things were taking off.

Clifton and I felt great about the church and just knew we had the very best people in the whole world. So, what could be the matter? We'd been able to acquire a building and Clifton had been working on it non-stop, with people helping as they were available.

The day I was going to lunch with my two lady friends, Clifton had been working at our new building with one of his best friends, who was also one of our favorite people in the church. We'd been given a building 25 x 100 square feet, worth over $210,000. Clifton had bought it for $1! He and another best friend in the church had found property to put it on, and they'd been working with the bank towards a loan. The paperwork was waiting at the bank for finalization. The building had to be disassembled and moved and it was hard work, but Clifton had done it all before, so he knew just how to do it.

The Spirit Warns the Church

There had been some contention with one of our board members, who was also Clifton's best friend and right-hand man. We didn't know what was wrong, but he wasn't himself towards us anymore.

The Holy Spirit knew exactly what was happening though, and He had given me a warning to share the Sunday morning before, concerning our building program. It was a portion of scripture from Nehemiah. I shared with our people that we needed to be aware that the devil was not going to just stand by and let us build without putting up a fight. I read from Nehemiah, chapter 4, where Sanballat and Tobiah conspired to fight against God's people to hinder the work for God. I found out later that a young lady in the church, who knew already of the conspiracy, was texting her friend in the children's ministry that I was up front talking about the two conspirators, whom she named. It would be funny, except it was a demonic attack which changed us forever.

Wounded In the House of My Friends

For this one man (Clifton's best friend and board member), to not talk to Clifton was an earth shaker. We had visited with him almost every day up to that point. He was over-the-top good to us, had been righteously angry at the way we'd been treated at the other church, and went above and beyond to help restore things to us. We loved him and his wife dearly. We trusted him. He was generous and had purchased many things for the church. This man had even secured a loan against his own home to help on the down payment we were going to need on the building we intended to buy. Ultimately, we were unable to buy that building, and our friend kept his money.

Clifton and I had noticed the change in him, and we'd prayed for him, and tried to talk to him. He wouldn't answer his phone. I had also tried to talk to his wife, but she wouldn't tell me anything. I was afraid they would leave, but she assured me that, no, they weren't leaving *their* church. I had no idea what was underneath that statement.

This man had fallen off the church building – off the roof – and hurt his ankle. I cooked food and we took it over to his house. His wife wasn't there, and he wouldn't even look at us. He didn't ask us to sit down. Nothing. He definitely would not allow us to pray for his healing.

The Other Shoe Drops

The big day was April 21, 2008. While I was at lunch that day, Clifton had received a phone call from another man in the church. This man was new in the things of God and new to our church. He told Clifton about the conspiracy against us, and said he thought we should know. Clifton immediately confronted one of the main instigators, our friend, who was working with him.

This man said there were stories about us using church money to furnish our home and buy things for our personal use. A swimming pool, lawn mower, etc. Clifton convinced this man that those things were not true. By the time I got there, our 'friend' was crying, begging for forgiveness. Then, the new member who'd called and given Clifton the heads up stopped by, and we all prayed. We laid hands on 'our friend.' He was headed to other the board member's home to tell that man that his pastors were innocent.

After that, he said that everything was okay, but it wasn't. Actually, the board member couple had convinced our worker friend that Clifton and I needed to be excommunicated from the church. That's why she had told me that they weren't leaving their church. They intended to kick us out!

On a Thursday night, while I was at worship practice and Clifton was making a trip to St. Louis to pick up a friend from the hospital, the conspirators were meeting at the home of one of my worship team members. They were deciding how to get rid of us. The two men: our best friends, our favorite people and men we held in highest esteem in front of the church, were going to an attorney the next morning!

"This is What's Going to Happen"

One of them was supposed to meet Clifton at the church on Friday morning to work, but he called and said he had "business" and would meet Clifton later that morning. Clifton went to the church office, by himself, to do some paperwork and this same man called him and made an announcement. He said, "This is what's going to happen." He would bring up accusations of theft and control before the church on Sunday morning, and we would be put out of the church.

How my husband made it through that day, I will never know. That was the beginning of a heartbreak that's indescribable. Clifton's heart nearly stopped, and someone who'd come into the church called me and wanted to call 911 for him. I talked to Clifton awhile on the phone, and he came home.

I personally begged several people to talk to us. I made phone calls to everyone involved. I sent emails which said, "Please talk to us!" I pleaded with the wife of our board member via email because she wouldn't answer her phone. That was before I knew what she'd done, or what she was telling everyone.

We had no idea what it was all about...

One of the couples who'd gone to the Thursday night meeting returned my call and agreed to come to our house and talk. They came over Friday night and told us that they'd thought that the Thursday night meeting was about the church, and that Clifton and I would be there. They were devastated by the accusations; they were crushed. They told us a little about the meeting. We talked, we prayed, and they left with peace. They said there was no prayer that Thursday night – nothing about it had seemed "Christian" to them. They believed we were telling them the truth; they said they believed they had been sent to Grace Family Outreach Church, and they were staying. I showed them the church's financial records.

At the beginning of the accusations, we lost most of our people. We walked in the following Sunday morning, not to a crowd of a 100+ people, but to a handful. Not one person who left ever came and asked us if the accusations were true. The couple at the bottom of all of it had acquired the church bank statements, but without the receipts and the other half of the church books, which we had, so there was a misunderstanding. It was an example of severe lack of communication. It was so sad, because all the questions could've been answered with better communication.

As the days and weeks passed, we used our own savings that we'd set aside for our basement to pay for the church and our own living. We weren't being paid by the church anymore and yet, somehow, all the bills were paid. Our small group became stronger; more unified. We were in one accord. Hallelujah!

Let It Go

The group that had made the accusations, then left, were seeking legal advice on how to get the building away from us. Clifton felt in his heart that in order to keep from dragging our people though a legal ordeal, he should just give them the building. We always believed that our people were precious and that we were their shepherds and supposed to be their protectors (1 Peter 5:2).

Clifton's name and the church's name were the only names on the legal contract. The building belonged to us. Clifton felt the Lord said, "Let it go," and let them have it. We went into the bank and spoke to the lender, the vice president, and explained the situation. We canceled the loan application for the ground we were purchasing for the church and told her that our plan was to give the building to the men.

It took me two whole years to figure out what'd happened with the people in the church and our best friends (we thought). Clifton and I sure didn't have any conflict with them. The whole ordeal blind-sided us. Those folks had gone through our School of Ministry and were our right-hand people. The betrayal was, by far, the worst heartbreak ever, worse than losing our home, our belongings, or even losing Ivan and the pets.

Betrayal pierces into the very lifeblood of a person. Ivan and the pets were in Heaven, but those men and women were still there, breathing out cruelty and accusations which simply were not true!

The Psalmist David wrote in Psalm 55:12-14 (KJV): *For it was not an enemy that reproached me; then I could have borne it :neither was it he that hated me that did magnify himself against me, then I would have hid myself from him. But it was thou, a man mine equal, my guide mine acquaintance. We took sweet counsel together, and walked into the house of God in company.*

Innocent

After we'd done all we knew to do, and we knew there were still accusations about the money, we took our books and receipts to an independent accountant, not a friend or anyone who would do us any favors, and paid them a large amount of money to go over everything with a fine-tooth comb. Their conclusion was that we had done nothing wrong at all. Nothing.

That whole devastating and heart-wrenching confusion could've been cleared up with just one question being asked and answered. To be honest, I should've had a financial meeting with the people involved before the misunderstanding started. My only excuse was that I was in grief and crushed over the losses we'd endured. I had my fault in this, but the church treasurer should've come to me. I wrote the checks because she asked me to do it. She said she was stressed with job and family matters, then she accused me of "taking the books away from her."

During those first few months, I cannot describe the pain that Clifton and I felt. We were pressed above measure. We were so devastated that we couldn't sleep, we couldn't live a normal life. We slept in intervals of only an hour or so at a time. My decorating came to a stop that day in April and never has been restarted. We walked the floors and we cried out to God. Again the Psalmist David knew how to describe the kind of anguish we felt in our souls.

In Psalm 69: 1-4 (KJV), David said: *Save me O God, for the waters have come into my soul, I sink in deep mire, where there is no standing: I am come into deep waters where the floods overflow me. I am weary of my crying, my throat is dried: my eyes fail while I wait for my God. They that hate me without a cause are more than the hairs of my head: they that would destroy me, being my enemies wrongfully are mighty"*

Verse 18, *"Draw nigh unto my soul and redeem it, deliver me because of my enemies.*

Every day God would lead me to scriptures like this. By the end of Psalm 69, David was rejoicing.

Verse 34: *Let the heaven and earth praise Him the seas and everything that moveth therein.*

We never have been ones to watch much Christian television. However, during those trying times, we had it on constantly, and it seemed that every message we heard was on the subject of betrayal and how to overcome it. Preachers who'd been through similar situations, and lived to tell about it, were being used by the Spirit of God to direct their words straight into our hearts for healing.

We were astounded at the way God was speaking to us and holding us in His arms. This happened every time I opened my Bible. I saw His love in a clearer, more powerful way than ever before (Psalms 27:10).

Threats came daily during those first few months. We heard that we were going to be arrested, and other debilitating horrors. It was overwhelming. I've never felt, before or since, like I did during those times – so isolated, so alone.

God spoke to me though. He called me His own. He showed me scriptures about my innocence and His unfailing faithfulness. He spoke to me to "stand still" and see His salvation. We decided to take the high road, and not do anything but trust God. He was clear He would take care of things. That was the only way we could survive.

Stand Still and See

Thankfully, we received phone calls from our friends across the United States and around the world. We had visitors at strategic times to minister life to us. Lynn and Shirley Osborne came from Kansas City, and Jim and Pam Kilpatrick visited us from Colorado. Both couples ministered to us, and also for us in our church.

God directed us to passages of scripture which brought life and divine help. Andrew Wommack called Clifton to encourage him, and said he'd received a phone call about us from one of the conspirators (the call was through his secretary, and the message was to call this man, but Andrew called Clifton directly instead). Andrew counseled us to "let it roll off." He knew us, and the people who have known us for decades knew that we certainly have faults, but not the kind of faults that would create the kind of accusations that were leveled against us.

But God, who is rich in mercy (see Ephesians 2:4), came to our rescue and brought back life to our very souls. It wasn't overnight, not by a long shot, but we kept going and believing God was leading us. Coming to terms with such an intimate betrayal was the most difficult part. We needed a new beginning, but I saw none ahead.

The Lord is near to those with a broken heart (see Psalm 147:3). I have to say that my greatest pain was not for my husband and me. My deepest anguish was (and still is) for the innocents who were damaged, the brand new ones in the Lord who ultimately fell through the cracks, and for my grandsons.

At the time, those boys had been abandoned by their dad. We had them in church and in the youth group, along with Cody. Our grandsons were receiving healing and learning forgiveness, and they loved their youth leaders. The boys were excited; playing music and singing. Among the boys, we had two on guitar, one on drums, and Cody played keyboard. They all enjoyed it so much.

When the whole destruction happened, it killed the boys' joy and zeal. They loved their grandparents and they knew what had happened wasn't right. It disillusioned them and to this day we're still picking up the pieces of their heartbreak. They love God though, and they know how to believe Him, so they'll be okay. They have roses to bloom too.

Chapter 18

The Dead Rose is Coming Back to Life

April through July 2008 was a time of walking through the valley of the shadow of death. By July, all our money was gone. When the people left, the money left. As I mentioned, we had to use our remodel money to keep things going. I wanted to get a job, not just for the money, but also to have a new perspective.

Our Grace Family Outreach people were wonderful. They were faithful, hanging in there with us, but I was still crushed. I couldn't get a handle on the losses. I needed to be around some new people who didn't know me at all.

The Lord reminded me of a scripture from the Bible, "Why sit we here till we die?" (2 Kings 7:3). I felt I was going to die if I didn't do something. I prayed about it on a Monday night towards the end of July. On Tuesday, a friend from church called me, wanting to know the qualifications to become an ordained minister. She was applying for a job as a hospice chaplain, and ordination was required. We talked about it, and before she hung up she said, "Geri, you should apply. They need a full time chaplain, and you would be perfect for the job."

I had been with her on a few hospice visits, as she was a volunteer for that organization. She gave me the phone number and I set up an interview. The next day, I drove down there and was hired on the spot. The administrator said she would have to run it by the owner of the company, but she felt I was the one they'd been looking for. I started work the first week of August, 2008. Now I was being paid to do what I had always done for free my entire ministry life. And they bought me a brand new car!

Now, I know this sounds strange, but that position was just what the doctor ordered. I started my job a broken hearted woman, full of despair. I didn't even know how dead I was, until I saw a ray of light the following year during a reunion with someone from our past.

Recently, I found some journal entries that spoke of the joy I received through the fellowship offered by our small (at the time) group of employees. I began to pour out my heart to those precious employees and patients, and Isaiah chapter 58 became a reality in my life. Spiritually, as we give out of our own hearts, and "satisfy the afflicted soul," light arises out of the darkness and we become like a "watered garden," whose waters fail not.

It is amazing how God gets us to where He wants us. There is a key though, and sadly I have found that most folks never find the key. Both believers and non-believers alike seem to take life as it comes, thinking they have no control: just a "que sera sera" (whatever will be, will be) type mindset.

A believer in the Lord Jesus Christ (a true disciple) will trust God and understand that He will do something for His children. I have found the key to a life of stability and blessing is to simply believe what He has said to us in His word. Somehow, I've learned over the years that God has a plan for me, and if I will just listen to Him and follow Him, I will see His glory in my life. And it does not matter what kind of messes we might get into…God is love, and He loves His kids!

After a year of working for Safe Harbor Hospice, God sent someone into my life to complete the healing that had begun. It was the end of summer 2009, when a former Lighthouse Christian School student and member of our Indiana church in the 1980's found us on Facebook and we reconnected.

Crissy Sanders

Clifton said to me, "Geri, look up Crissy Sanders' website, she has Gloria Copeland coming to teach at her conference." We were astounded! We had moved to Colorado in 1995, and had only a small amount of contact with her before then. She and her husband, Dennis, had done some pastoral work in a church in Paoli, our home town. Then they left Paoli, and through a series of youth pastorates and other church work, they ended up in Terre Haute as senior pastors over the past ten years. When I viewed their website, I was ecstatic to see the work being done by this little student we'd taught in our Lighthouse Christian School so many years ago. She and her brother were raised with my children, and we all knew each other. Her mother had been a dear friend who'd prayed with me at 5 o'clock in the morning all one summer. After our prayer time at the church, we would walk two miles and talk about our families and God.

Crissy contacted Clifton and me and invited us to be her guests and to come to Terre Haute to the Gloria Copeland conference. Crissy was teaching at the conference too. She probably thought she was just inviting her former pastors, and intended to honor us, but she had no idea what we'd been through, and what we were still going through.

This is a beautiful example of something life-altering and relevant to every believer. Crissy was obeying the spirit of God. Even I didn't realize what was about to happen. First of all, I didn't realize how shattered I was, still, over the betrayal of our so-called "friends" and the split of the church. I didn't realize until later, after the invitation to the meeting in Terre Haute, how dead I'd become and how much fire I'd lost.

Royalty

From the first moment we arrived in Terre Haute, Indiana, we were treated like royalty. Crissy and her staff catered to us, and honored us practically to the point of embarrassment. She called us to the microphone after an introduction that raised us up so high. Crissy publicly honored us as much as anybody, anywhere, on any platform, had ever done. She was so thankful for the Word of God we'd sown into her life at a critical time, and she'd never forgotten it.

We were given a seat on the platform directly behind Gloria Copeland and CeCe Winans. Later, after the service, we were invited into a private room where photos were being taken, and Crissy included us all the way. It was humbling and amazing.

Gloria taught on Mark 11:23-24. I'd heard her teach in Charlotte, North Carolina, way back in the early 1980's. Her message was the same; her testimony was the same. She and Ken were healthy, taking no medicine, living the life of God. She gave their ages and I was taken aback, and yet, they do get older, like the rest of us.

Crissy gave us the testimony of how it came about that Sister Copeland was there. It all started with a word from a prophet – a word that she would teach alongside Gloria Copeland one day. Years later, God spoke to Crissy to call Gloria, so Crissy did and spoke with Gloria's secretary. The arrangements were made and adhered to.

As for me, the treatment I received under Crissy's ministry was life changing. The love of God was overflowing, the Spirit of God ministered to me in such a powerful way, and I was revived, restored, and refreshed. I came away from the conference not being able to even articulate the transformation that had happened on the inside of me (Clifton felt the same way. We talked about it as much as we could, but it was something that, at that time, couldn't be expressed in words).

Crissy invited me to speak at a couple of spring conferences, and it was one of the highlights of my ministry. Our church supported her last mission trip to Africa, and we've invited Crissy to our church to speak for us.

Crissy is thankful that we sponsored her in church camps and our Christian School. She thanks us for seed sown so many years ago, but she will never know what she gave to us that weekend in 2009!

Thank you, Crissy!

Chapter 19

Kelly

In October 2010, came the event which changed our lives forever. I can't publish a book without including this story. On Saturday, October 16, about 4 o'clock in the afternoon, our eldest son Kelly was killed in a tractor accident on his farm in Indiana. We got the call about five o'clock in the afternoon. Just a little while before the phone call came, I was standing at my kitchen sink and I had a sharp, piercing pain in my chest. I mentioned it to Clifton, and went and sat down in a chair. Clifton's phone rang. I knew something was wrong, and I kept trying to find out what it was. He finally took a break to say, "Kelly is dead!"

Until you've lost a child, there is no way to understand the effect news like that has on a mother's heart. Clifton went back to the phone to try to find out what'd happened. I hurriedly walked back down our lane to the woods, where there's an acre clearing. It is beautiful and park-like, with a huge oak tree in the corner. I have a log I sit on and talk to God. I've found solace there in my times of dread and fear.

God, Why?

I was mad. My precious Phoebe Westie went with me, trying to console me. I yelled, "God, how much is one family supposed to endure?!" I was in disbelief over the tragedy. I understood the Psalmist David's words as he cried out in agony in Psalm 55:4-7, KJV: *My heart is sore pained within me: and the terrors of death are fallen upon me, Fearfulness and trembling are come upon me, and horror hath overwhelmed me. And I said, "O that I had wings like a dove! For then I would fly away and be at rest. Lo, then I would wander off and remain in the wilderness.*

I was numb, and yet the pain was so sharp, so deep, so raw. It was so overwhelming that I didn't think I could keep on breathing.

Kelly was killed instantly. His body couldn't be shown at the funeral home due to head injuries. 'Multiple skull fractures' they called it. His head was crushed under the weight of the heavy-duty tractor. We took our old photos from over the years to display at the memorial service. His widow (they'd been married less than two years) had many pictures and videos which she provided.

The planning for the service was fast, and I don't remember very much about even getting to Indiana. We left on Sunday morning. Our daughter Kami, who lived in Indiana at the time, was filling in for us with the situation. She had ridden in the vehicle which came to take Kelly away. It took five hours to recover his body from the accident. I'm still not sure why. I haven't seen the place where it happened.

Kami held Kelly's hand, even though he was in a body bag. I don't think I could have done that emotionally. Kami is strong. God gave her the strength to do what was needed. She went to the funeral home with Callie, Kelly's widow, and they were on the phone with Clifton, making the plans. Callie said Kelly had expressed a desire to be cremated. Harvey, the director and owner of the funeral home, allowed us to touch Kelly and say our last goodbyes. He was wrapped in a sheet on a table and still had his boots and jeans on. I prayed for him to be raised from the dead. I spoke life into his body. Clifton told me later he did the same thing. Kelly's body remained still and cold.

Maybe Kelly chose to stay in Heaven? I don't know very much about how to figure that all out. Some people think they have it all down pat – just how and why things happen. A long time ago, I had all the answers. Now, I have no answers. The only thing I know – for sure – is that God loves me, He lives in me, and He is forever faithful. His mercies are new every morning (see Lamentations 3:22-23). He has refreshing for us every day. So I trust Him, rain or shine.

A Perfect Baby

I've had to stop and breathe several times during this chapter. There is so much to say. As a baby he was beautiful, perfect, and the joy of our lives. He had a lot of reddish blonde hair.

The doctor called it 'strawberry blonde.' His skin was smooth and white, and he was a sweet and wonderful baby. He slept good, awoke every four hours to eat, and didn't give us a minute's trouble. People told me I didn't know what it was like to have a little baby, because Kelly was so good. (Actually, all my kids were like that. They slept from the time they came home from the hospital. They were all very good babies.)

Kelly exhibited happiness from the time he was very little. When he was born he was smiling and laughing! He grew up loving life and adventure and got the most out of every day. He was the "life of the party," and he *was* the party. He lit up the room, and I'm not just saying that because he's gone. I'm not trying to make him better than he was.

Kelly had a way, a presence about him. He was able to make people feel important. He was anointed. A friend of Clifton's made a comment at the memorial service that Kelly would walk across the parking lot to shake his hand and visit, with the attitude that he had all day. Anytime people were involved, Kelly was never in a hurry. He loved people.

When Kelly was three years old, we had our second son, Dustin. Clifton and I feared Kelly would feel left out, so Clifton took Kelly with him everywhere he went. They became buddies. Clifton bought Kelly a pony when he was three. Dilly was its name. Kelly wanted to be a cowboy even before that. As soon as he could walk, he put on his dad's boots and cowboy hat, so we got him his own boots and hat. He loved it.

Kelly was smart in school, and a joy to his teachers. He did get into some "just being a boy" fights and mischief, but nothing major until high school, when he was expelled for drinking on the first day of his senior year. There were many who did this, but only four got caught and Kelly was one of them. I always told my kids that whenever they did wrong at school, they would get caught – that was God's way of helping them.

He came home from school that day and said, "Mom, can we take a walk?" I'd always told him, "Kelly, I'm your best friend. I'll help you any way I can." So he told me the horror story about the drinking. I remember starting off my answer by saying, "Nobody's dead, we will work through this." And we did, but his drinking became more than just a passing teenage phase.

An Excellent Athlete

Kelly was an excellent athlete, talented in both baseball and football. Once he received a visit from a college baseball scout who wanted Kelly to accept an athletic scholarship. Another time, Kelly was contacted by the football coach at Indiana University, who tried to get Kelly on a football scholarship. Kelly turned them all down – he'd started building bridges with Clifton, and he was making good money. The baseball scout said Kelly made more money than he did.

We lived in Florida when he was little, and I sent him to swimming lessons when he was just four years old. Kelly learned to swim the very first lesson and he was jumping off the high dive at six years old. When he was older, I remember the family had all gone to his baseball team's award and swimming party. When they announced the Most Valuable Player award, everyone there knew who'd been the most valuable player, but when the coach called Kelly's name to come forward for the trophy, Kelly looked around at everyone and had the most incredulous look of surprise on his face. "ME?" It was priceless!

Kelly carried that attitude throughout his entire life. He was always thankful, always appreciative of any favor he received, even when it was his due. He showed respect and honor to his bosses and did the best job he could. That is why he was promoted time after time. Kelly was a "company man" like his dad, but he always looked out for his men and made sure they had everything they needed.

In 1987, Kelly graduated high school and went to work with his dad. Clifton and I had prayed about some extra outside income because we were down in attendance and finances at the Lighthouse. Right after that, Clifton was approached by an old boss who wanted him to come back to work and build two bridges for him that summer. We got a camper and we all went to Terre Haute while Clifton taught Kelly how to do that kind of work. Kelly learned how to build bridges from beginning to end – top to bottom – and he made a lot of money. Kelly worked his way up from laborer to superintendent in just a few years.

Overwhelming Pain

Kelly met his wife at church. They got married and had four boys. A baby girl, Kelsey JoyAnne, was born in 1993, but went to Heaven the same day. Great grief struck me at that time. I held her. She was a full term, perfect little baby girl, except for the birth defect: encephalitis. The top of her head didn't close, but with the little hat they had on her head, it didn't show. I didn't look at it. I just held her for a few minutes to say goodbye. She was beautiful.

Feeling Kelly's and Darlene's pain was overwhelming. We knew about the problem early in Darlene's pregnancy, but we had believed for a miracle.

Kelly and the baby's doctor, Terry Nofziger, cried in each other's arms from the depths of their souls. Kelly and Darlene's little family came home from the hospital to stay at my house for a few days. Darlene asked, "Could they come?" In spite of their loss, Kelly and Darlene were at church the very next service, on the front row, with their hands high in the air, worshiping the Lord. I sat in the back. They seemed to be doing better than I was. Darlene read her little white Bible every day.

The Truth Comes

I was very upset about what'd happened. Then one day Lynn Osborne called. When I answered the phone and heard it was him, I said, "Do you want to talk to Clifton?" He said, "No Geri, I want to talk to you." He helped me a lot. He shared about God's love for us, and said that the baby's death was NOT God's idea. Something happened inside me that day that caused me to see the truth – that precious little baby was with Jesus, and we would all be okay. Someday soon, we'd see her again.

But Kelly blamed himself for the baby's death. He wasn't "living right," he said. At that time, we didn't know he was a heavy drinker. Alcoholism is a disease. It's hereditary. Kelly was a "high functioning" alcoholic, so he worked hard every day, but drank too much.

Clifton and I loved our son more than the breath in our bodies (we feel that way about all our kids). In our children's teenage years, we'd had some serious marriage issues and were all but divorced. That was tremendously painful for Kelly. His drinking started during that time, and he never stopped. He talked to me about it once and told me he'd tried to stop drinking several times, but it was a plague to him until the day he died.

I loved him with all my heart, and felt we were always close, but he was especially close to his "Daddy." They had a multifaceted relationship. They shared many of the same interests: carpentry, concrete work, and horses. Also, they both had the same sense of humor, and laughed at things other people didn't think were amusing. Kelly was always funny and his boys have his sense of humor too.

A Big Heart

Kelly had a heart as big as the whole world. He loved people, he was generous and kind, and he was an honest horse trader. Everyone liked Kelly. He had lots of friends. His talent for horse training was developed through years of trial and error and help from his dad, who is a natural animal trainer. I used to say Clifton had "horse blood flowing through his veins."

Kelly had a vision of Jesus when he was eight years old. He knew God was real. He was saved and baptized, and he knew the power of the Holy Spirit. I cannot explain why he left his family and went against everything we believed in: what he knew in his heart was right and wrong.

Drugs and alcohol destroy people's lives every day, but I always thought, "Not my child." I had scriptures that were illuminated to me, and I believed that Kelly would see the truth and return to his family. He did return a few times during the first three years of the separation – he moved the family to Missouri, left them there, and returned three times. But after he left the third time, he married "the other woman."

Tormented

I know Kelly loved his boys, and was proud of them. We'd had a discussion on the phone the eve of his home-going. I was adamant. I tried to convince Kelly that they loved him, because he said the boys hated him. I knew Kelly was tormented about his children not being with him. He'd actually built them a place to stay, a remodeled space in the upstairs of the farmhouse where he lived with his new wife. He thought they would come and live with him, but they didn't and he was hurt. Kelly had filed for custody of the kids in the divorce papers, but the kids chose not to live with him: they loved their mother, and it would've added pain on top of unbearable pain if they had left her too.

That Friday night, I tried to explain to Kelly that his boys were hurt: they weren't mad at him, just brokenhearted. The whole family was upset. Everyone had been forced to work at overcoming the circumstances created by Kelly's choices. I know for sure that both Kelly and his four boys believed that someday, they would have a relationship again. And some things had already gotten better: Kelly had done graduation parties for the boys, and he'd come and got them the Christmas before he died and brought them back to Indiana for two weeks. They'd played laser tag and he had taken them paint-balling and given them a good Christmas vacation. I have a picture of the five of them at my house, right before they left for Indiana.

Darlene and Kelly were married for twenty years. Darlene has never once disrespected me, or shown anything but support for our ministry and our family. We love her like a daughter. She had realized the things she needed to change to save her marriage, but as far as Kelly was concerned, it was too late.

I begged the other woman to leave him alone, believing that without her influence, Kelly would see the truth and return to his family, but Kelly thought he loved the other woman. What can a parent do? After their marriage, I accepted the situation and did the best I could. Neither Kelly nor his new wife ever told us that they'd gotten married. We found out through a family member.

An Act of Mercy

As I pondered the loss I was experiencing, God spoke to me. He said, "This was an act of mercy." I didn't understand that then, and I'm still thinking about it today. I do see some spiritual benefits to going to Heaven as opposed to staying down here and facing the challenges of life. In March of 2010,

Kelly told me about some severe pain in his shoulders, which needed surgery. He had no money and no insurance for medical treatment. He didn't have any assets to fall back on. In fact, the day he died, he owned nothing. Not even the truck he drove.

The day Kelly told me about his shoulders, I made a journal entry that he "broke my heart." We had talked about many things that day. He came to my mother's (his grandmother's) 80th birthday party later that week, and that was the last time I ever saw him. I'd been scheduled to see him in July that year, but his phone was dead, our wires got crossed, and I missed him. Kelly called me (after we'd missed each other while I was on the interstate heading back to Missouri), and we talked on the phone. He was so disappointed that I hadn't waited for him to get back. I had driven to his house after I couldn't reach him, but had to leave. That episode has bothered me, but I had Kami's kids with me, and we were going to Missouri.

Kelly and I sent text messages to each other to keep up on the news. He was so interesting to talk to. He always had funny stories. I texted him every week with a message of how much I loved him, and I also texted his boys.

God Is Faithful

Kelly was in the process of building a barn to use as an inside arena – it was a dream he'd had – and he was training horses. Business wasn't good enough to be full-time, so he was also going to start a new job on the Monday after the tragic accident.

When I talked to him that Friday night, we covered a lot of territory. I see God in it. God is so faithful. Had I not talked to Kelly that night, I would be much more distraught than I am. I'd also called him that morning and left a message, asking him to help Dustin, his brother. Dustin had called me, and I just couldn't do anything, being five hours away. I called Kelly because I knew he would do something. That's the way he was. Anytime I called him about any problem, he would take care of it if it was within his power. And if not, he found someone, or some way to help and fix it.

That had been our relationship all the while he was growing up. I didn't realize how much he was like that; how dependable he was when the chips were down. He reported to me that night, "I took care of Bro, Mom. Don't worry, he's coming out here." He was so happy that he'd relieved me of some stress. He had me cracking up on the phone with his stories.

We also were very serious on a couple of matters. I thank God, every time I think of this situation, that we did talk about his kids, and I was able to assure him they loved him. We laughed, I cried, we got aggravated at each other, but in the end, his last words to me were, "I love you, Mom, and tell Daddy I love him." Whichever one he talked to, he always said to tell the other one of us that he loved us. I treasure those words and I treasure that conversation. It was a gift from God.

The Memorial Service

We asked Gerald Reliford (from Columbia, Kentucky) and Ed Shirley (from Conifer, Colorado) to speak at the memorial, the Celebration of Life service we held for Kelly. Gerald's message was so amazing. I will never forget it. He said the service was about two men. He proceeded to give the salvation message about Jesus, and then he spoke of Kelly. Gerald and LaVerne Reliford have been close friends of ours since Cody was a baby. We've walked with each other through some very difficult circumstances (including situations with our children through their teen years and beyond), ministered in each other's churches, and have a long list of stories and testimonies which we laugh at now. At the time, we cried, and things weren't funny. Gerald and LaVerne had visited us in Colorado. We share some miracle testimonies. We wanted them at the service. They were a strength to us, and we are forever grateful.

Ed Shirley was the other man we asked to share at the service. He was Kelly's pastor when the family lived in Colorado in 2005. We first met Ed and Mona in 1995, when we moved to Colorado. As soon as we met them, we clicked in the spirit. Mona is a dear friend to me. We decided at that time we were "family." Their son, Adam, flew out to Indiana to be with us and show his love for Kelly. He was also a true friend. The Shirleys have always given above and beyond. In years past, they came to Indiana and put on rodeo clinics at Kelly's farm in Hardinsburg, when Kelly's boys were little. The boys had just started bull riding, and that training was invaluable. Ed's son, Tim, is a champion bucking horse rider and Casey, Kelly's second son, has become a champion bull rider, a member of the PBR (Professional Bull Riders).

With the foundation laid by Pastor Gerald, Pastor Ed built on it, and after painting a beautiful picture of our son, proceeded to give an invitation for salvation. The building was packed to capacity. Many had to be turned away. Both rooms were full, but Ed could only see one room, and he estimated later that 40-50 hands went up for salvation. Well, PRAISE THE LORD! Kelly would have been overjoyed.

Another thing Kelly would've been amazed by were the number of people who came to show respect and honor his memory. He would've had outstretched arms, saying, "What? All this for me?" The stream of people who came with stories of Kelly's kindness towards them, his generosity, his sincere care for them – it was seemingly unending. Clifton and I couldn't believe it and neither could the funeral home owner.

Clifton and I stood for seven and a half hours and greeted the people. The funeral director said at least 1,500 folks came through on Monday night for the viewing, and many had to be turned away. People were lined up for blocks and cars backed up for miles that couldn't get in. The police were summoned to direct traffic. Yes, my Kelly was definitely a traffic stopper!

The next day the funeral was standing room only, and people told me later that they wanted to come, but couldn't even get near the funeral home. Friends flew or drove in from Colorado, Tennessee and other states, and calls came in from literally all over the world. We had American friends in England and India who called, and friends in Ireland and other places who are continuing with prayerful support. We received hundreds of texts, letters, emails, cards, phone calls, and six months later, they were still continuing to pour in. Kelly was loved, and it seemed we were loved also!

When someone passes on, many times "sainthood" emerges for that person. I am, by no means, saying that Kelly was a saint. I knew his faults when he was living on earth. I haven't forgotten the difficult, tumultuous times we had during his days of making decisions about his family that all but killed me and his dad. However, there was a deep love between us. Kelly was a strong believer in Jesus, and I know he prayed. He told me he did. His heart was torn about his family, but I know for sure he believed that in the future he would have a good relationship with his boys. Darlene also had a special place in his heart, as the mother of his children.

The Dream

Soon after Kelly's passing, Kami had a dream about Kelly. In her dream, there were four of us family members standing outside, and we were all talking about Kelly. Suddenly, we saw him standing there with us.

Kelly was transparent, and he said he'd had to get permission to come and tell us something. Kami said he looked at us and said, "I am so sorry you are sad." He said he was fine, and for us not to worry about him. He was happy.

Kelly said he had something in his pocket for Kami. It was a handkerchief of his Kami had wanted. He said, "Here, Sis, I thought you might like this." He said, "I girly-ed it up for you." It had ruffles sewn around it. It was his turquoise kerchief. Kami had found a belt buckle in her jacket pocket, and Kelly said he wanted his dad to have that. It wasn't the buckle he had won, it was an older one. He had written his name on the back with a black marker. So like him.

Kelly had won a belt buckle and a jacket for earning the most points on his horse at various horse shows over a year's time. It was the Ranch Horse Association high-point championship. Kelly had told me about it on the phone that night. There was an awards banquet in November and Clifton and I agreed to "co-receive" his awards with his widow. The whole family went. I walked into the banquet hall to see Kelly's award jacket on a hanger beside two huge poster-sized photos of him on his horse. That's when it hit me – like a ton of bricks. Kelly was gone. I cried for days. I was not going to see him again in this life.

In Kami's dream, when Kelly said he had to go, he said he only had permission for a short time. Kelly hugged her, telling her goodbye. Kami said it was the best hug she'd ever had. She could feel his muscles, his arms around her. She could smell him and she said it was so very real.

There was a second dream immediately following this one, and he took her to Heaven with him. She saw that he had a huge bed, covered with a blue silk bedspread. He stretched out on it with his hands behind his head, smiling, and he told her he could do anything he wanted to do in his new home. He took her around to see other people. He wanted her to know he was happy. He was home.

The dreams were a great comfort to me. To be honest though, some days I didn't think I would make it to the end of the day. Some days I still don't. I've come to realize that some roses bloom again only in Heaven.

To My Son

January 11, 1969 was a day of days for this Mom,

Remembering with joy the day you were born.

So beautiful was your skin and strawberry hair,

Your good looks were the talk of the OB Ward there.

Your little boy life was adventurous and fun,

You built a fort in our woods where battles were won.

As a teen your talents on the field shown bright,

You were a football star, and pitched the baseball just right.

Most Valuable Player was the award,

Everything about you was a gift from the Lord.

Building roads and bridges you were the man in charge,

And your kindness helped others; your heart was so large.

You were funny; they say the class clown,

But also a true friend- the best around.

Your gift for horse training by all was seen,

A champion at the horse shows, following your dream.

A proud dad, you raised your boys with love,

Giving them all you could with help from above.

Now I miss you, Kelly, we weren't prepared for the news,

That day in October when we lost you.

We long to see your face and kiss you again,

This time never to part, Amen!

In loving memory of Kelly Edward Coulter
January 11, 1969 ～ October 16, 2010

Chapter 20

Dimes

After saying our goodbyes to Kelly, we headed back to Missouri and started trying to find the "new normal." I was still off work, but I was already pre-registered and scheduled to go to a meeting for chaplains in St Louis. The topic was "Near Death Experiences." The meeting was only ten days after the accident. I thought a day out with friends might be good for me, so I went.

Crazy Woman

I was still a little fragile to be doing something like that, especially with the title, but I went, I listened, I cried, and was ready to leave as soon as the meeting was over. Right before the dismissal, a woman got up to share her story. As she spoke, I remember thinking, "She's crazy," and I wanted to leave so badly. This woman was saying something about people finding dimes after a loved one had passed, but I didn't listen to too many of the details. All I heard was "finding dimes" and "when people would hear the story, then they too would start finding dimes."

We left. No one said anything about the crazy woman or the dimes. I went home, and within a day or two, I found a dime at the bottom of the washer. I didn't think a thing about it at the time. I took it out. Then I found another one between my flat tablecloth and my hand-crocheted tablecloth on our big dining table. That's when I remembered the dime story. My grandson Colten was there when I found the one on the table, and I said, "How did that dime get there?" He said, "Mammaw, here's a dime by my foot." We were both astonished.

My daughter Kami came over to our house from Indiana, and in a few days my middle son, Dustin, came down and he said he'd found a dime by his tire as he was getting in his car to drive. The four of us had gone to breakfast: Clifton, me, Kami, and Dustin. I was getting back into my seat in the car when I noticed a dime there. It happened then, and continues to happen, on a regular basis.

After a while, a penny began to appear with the dimes. This happens to all of us. When Dustin got home from that trip, he texted me and said when he walked into his house, he saw a dime on the TV. I said, "What did you do?" He said, "I said, 'Praise the Lord,' and put it in my pocket."

I asked the other chaplains who'd been at the meeting if they remembered the name of the place where we went, or the names of any of the people we saw, and none of them remembered anything except the dime story. I did track down the "crazy lady" who told that story, and called her in March of 2011. Her name was Suzie.

The Original Dime Story

Suzie told me this story: a young mother had a little boy named Shawn, who was five years old. She would give him a dollar and tell him, "This is for being such a good son." Shawn would then go into his room, dig into his change jar, and bring her back a dime, saying, "Here, Mommy, this is for being such a good mom."

Later on, Shawn was killed in a school bus accident. One day, after the funeral, his mom was cleaning out his bedroom, and began to find dimes under his shirts. Soon, she was finding them all over the house. As a Christian, she asked God what it meant. He brought her memory back to Shawn giving her the dime and saying, "This is for being such a good mom." The dimes were a sign to her, a real comfort.

I cried when I heard this. The dimes were a sign to me too. Over the years, I have received such great comfort in finding so many dimes (even though I still don't understand it).

My relationship with Kelly had been strained over the past four years. We'd had no estrangement or hard feelings at the time of his death, and we'd gradually moved past the new relationship with his second wife. No, my grief with him was over his boys – occasionally, we would talk about them, but he was in such pain over that situation that we didn't dwell on it a lot. He would've loved to see Casey and Koix ride bulls and Colten play football. (Dustin Lee, the oldest son, didn't ride bulls, and was out of school by that time.)

Kelly was so proud of all the boys. "My boys," he would say. When he put on the graduation parties for the two who graduated, he had Cody and his band come to entertain everyone, which was another God-thing for Kelly to see Cody's talents and be so proud of him. From Cody's viewpoint, their relationship had never been a pleasant one, that was, until Kelly invited Cody's band to travel up to Indiana to stay at his place. Cody said that when the band arrived at 3 a.m., Kelly came out to greet everyone in his underwear and cowboy boots!

I Share the Dime Story

When I tracked Suzie down, I told her about my experiences, and she said my story was phenomenal. Suzie said she'd never heard of someone finding so many dimes so quickly (we'd found almost two hundred dimes between October and March). She asked me to come to St. Louis and tell my 'dime story,' so I did in April, 2011.

I ended my testimony in St. Louis with an astounding story that had just happened. I'd gone to Terre Haute to speak at a conference there. My daughter, Kami, went with me, and we were sitting at the product table where I had my CDs and sets of teachings for sale. A preacher, who Clifton and I had only met the year before, came over to our table before the meeting. As he approached us, he bent down and picked up something off the carpet. He laid it on the table. It was a dime. Kami and I looked at each other, and he looked at us, like, "What?" I smiled and said, "I'll tell you later." So, when we got up to the auditorium, I found him and told him the dime story.

The next morning, a Saturday, was the day we were all leaving. That morning, he motioned to me from across the room. I walked over, and he had a story for me. Now, I want to remind you that everyone had been staying in our motel rooms since Thursday and it was now Saturday morning. He told me when he got up that morning and his feet hit the floor, there was something on the carpet beside his bed. He handed it to me. It was a bright, shiny "Golden Dollar." He said, with tears in his eyes, "My mother is in Heaven." I said, "Well, thank you for being such a good son."

Now I know what many of you are thinking, but I can't help it. All I can do is tell everyone what happened. I am not a flake. I'm a solid 'Word woman.' I base my beliefs on Jesus Christ and the Bible. But what can I say? It's a legitimate experience, and it really happened to me.

A Dime From Heaven

Dimes continue to show up. It amazes me, because I've never found a dime when I was purposely looking for one. They appear, mostly, when I'm distraught about a situation – not always though. Sometimes I find one randomly, for no reason. When that happens, I'm blessed and comforted, and it always makes me smile...or cry.

In January of 2012, Kelly would've been 43 years old (he was born in 1969). That year, on a day close to his birthday, I was working my hospice job and was sinking down with sadness to the point I had to take a break. I have a remedy for dealing with overwhelming grief and pressure: I go to Sonic and purchase a Cherry Limeade (my good friend, Denise Capra, showed me these drinks back in 1990) and I go somewhere quiet and take my time drinking it, praying, and breathing. I get the big Route 44 size, and I make sure it's between 2 and 4 p.m., so I get the half-price discount.

I ordered my drink. My purse was in the back seat, and I actually had to get out of the car to get it. When I opened the door, there on the pavement beside the car, was a dime. There was no small stir in my heart when I saw it. I picked it up. I'd never looked at the date on any of the dimes before, but that day I did.

What I saw next left me so taken aback that I got my glasses and looked again, and I still couldn't believe my eyes! When the young girl brought me my drink, I asked her to read me the date on the dime. She said, with assurance, "1969." It absolutely blew me away! Now, I ask you, was it a coincidence that a dime dated 1969 – a 43-year-old dime – was lying beside my car the afternoon I was grieving about Kelly and his 43rd birthday?

The comfort of our Father God is beyond comprehension. I don't understand it. And I must add, a few years ago I would've never believed that our loved ones in Heaven could be responsible for such encounters. That 1969 dime held then, and still holds today, more significance than I can humanly articulate.

I took the dime to a friend who owns a pawn shop and asked him if he would put it on a chain for me. I told him my story. He helped me far beyond his professional responsibility – Jeff is his name. He had a bezel and a unique chain and he put it all together with that dime and it's been around my neck ever since.

Sometimes I'm "led" to share the story when people ask about my dime necklace, or make a comment about it. Or sometimes when someone is telling me about how they lost a child or a loved one: then I sense I should tell them the "dime story," as we've grown to call it.

I don't know how it happens, but after I tell them the dime story and what all happened to me, they immediately start to find dimes.

God is a Father

Soon after I began wearing the dime necklace, I stopped at a little roadside sandwich place on one of my hospice routes. Edna, the waitress, noticed the dime and made a comment. I always have it shining. I told her about it, and she wept, and said her daughter had passed away of a drug overdose seven years ago. She told me of a dream she had of her daughter. It was funny that the restaurant stayed empty the whole time Edna was talking – it was just me and her. I love how God arranges things for us. Smile. I prayed for her and was able to minister love and hope to her. Her daughter had loved the Lord, but got sidetracked and lost her life to drugs.

I want to interject here that a lot of "religion" today would have you believe there was no hope for that dead girl – she went straight to hell because of her bad behavior. To be truthful, some legalistic, religious people I know thought that about my precious son, when he passed. They did and they still do. However, I happen to know God better than that.

I talked to Edna about her daughter. I explained that God is a Father and loves us just like we love our children and just like our children, who will always be our children, we will *always* be His once we receive Jesus and are born again.

She was the first person I told why I wear the dime around my neck. The next time I walked into the restaurant, she came running up to me and said, "Oh, I've been waiting for you. You'll never believe this!" She proceeded to say that after I left the week before, she had swept the entire restaurant before closing. The next morning, when she arrived, there were two dimes lying on the floor in her path. She was ecstatic! I saw her a few more times before I no longer traveled that route. The dime story changed her life. She will never be the same.

My Hairdresser

Patti, my hairdresser, is someone I've known the whole time I've been in Missouri. She was part of my healing during the Kelly tragedy, and all my tragedies actually. I went to her initially because she said she would love to get her hands on my hair. I'd been in her shop for a massage, and had told the massage therapist that I couldn't find a hairdresser I liked, and had been driving back to Indiana to get my hair done every three months. A girl's gotta have good hair!

Well, I went to Patti, and kept going. She lets me talk or honors my quietness, either way, and always sends me out lookin' good! When I told her about the dimes, she told me the story of the tragic death of her grandmother. A few days later she called me, crying but ecstatic! She said she'd been thinking about her grandmother all day, and was sad. Then, while she was standing in a Wal-Mart checkout line, she happened to look down, and to her utter surprise and amazement, there was a dime beside her feet. Patti has found several dimes since that first one and she keeps them in a zipper pouch; twelve of them so far, and the dimes always come when she's sad, thinking about her sweet grandmother.

Skeptical Steve

One time, Steve, an analytical friend of mine, asked me about the dime around my neck. I told him the dime story, and by that time, I had several testimonies of others finding dimes too. Steve was skeptical. Skeptical Steve. I told him, "You'll probably find a dime too." He'd recently lost his sister and his dad to cancer. Steve didn't think so, but he didn't want to argue with me. I had also told him about the pennies, which regularly accompany our dimes. (I don't tell that part to everybody. I try to keep it short.)

Steve's wife, Gwen, knows me, believes me, and heard our conversation. She called me a day or so later and said that when they got home that evening, Steve went out on their deck to grill. They have a little table out there that never has anything on it. Steve and Gwen don't normally leave change lying out, but that evening, there on that deck table, were dimes and pennies! They had no explanation at all.

Once, I had an in-home hospice patient, and I stopped by when all her daughters were there. They were going through mom's jewelry, and I happened to see some vintage earrings made from mercury, "lady head" dimes from long ago. As the visit went on, I ended up at their kitchen table with one of the daughters. I was led to tell her about the dime story, my dimes and my special necklace. She'd been very sad and tearful over her grandmother's passing a few years earlier; she'd spent most of her growing-up time with her. We talked for a bit. After the visit was over and I was driving away from their home, the daughter called me and said, "I have to ask you. Did you put a dime under my soda? Because there's one there now and I know it wasn't there when I put the can down on the counter!"

Recently, Clifton was in the hair salon (yes, a salon) where he gets free haircuts. Smile. A sweet lady who loves us had heard all the gossip years ago coming from the church we had to leave back in 2006. We'd gone in for his haircut during that time, and she brought us outside and said, "I've heard all the gossip and rumors, and I want you to know – I don't believe a word of it, and you will never again pay for a haircut here!" So, that's where he goes. Anyway, Clifton was in there recently, and saw a dime on the floor where the hairdresser had been walking between rooms. He pointed it out, and she said, "How did that get there? I've been back and forth all morning, and didn't see it." Clifton told her he would bring me in to tell our dime story. So, we did. Later, we ran into her and had lunch together, and she told us how she'd been finding dimes ever since that day. She lost a brother too young.

At work my boss, Amy, had me tell the dime story at one of our weekly meetings. People were asking me about my necklace, and some knew the story, but she wanted me to tell it to everybody. After a few days, an employee messaged me, and said she'd gone to her recently deceased brother's grave, and as she walked across the gravel to his gravestone, she saw a dime, right there in her path! She needed the assurance that her brother was okay.

These stories continue on a regular basis. I've started including the "dime story" in some of my ladies' meetings, as the Holy Spirit leads. I've also begun to share my revelations on Heaven. I'm growing bolder, and I don't care if folks believe me or not.

Chapter 21

Grieving and Honoring Kelly

Going through that first Mother's Day without hearing from my son was an experience I'd never had before, and I never want to feel that bad again. When I woke up that morning, without warning, a wave of grief swept over me. As I got out of bed and prepared to go to church, I couldn't talk. Clifton and Cody talked to me, but I didn't answer and they didn't seem to notice. They chatted all the way to church. I'd put on an old dress, and didn't even try to look good. It was a new level of despair. We got through the service. Clifton called me up to the front, and I managed to say something. I just wanted to go home.

I was in my kitchen the following Saturday, home alone for the first time I could remember since Kelly had been gone. I was cleaning, and needed my worship CD's, which were in the car. (I only listen to Christian music. It comforts me, and keeps me going.) I was too lazy to go get them, so I looked around for a CD.

In my junk basket, I saw a CD with the name "Kid Rock" on it. I was surprised, and thought, "How did that get there?" I knew

Kelly loved Kid Rock, but I did NOT like that kind of music. Nevertheless, I put it in the CD player, which was strongly out of character for me.

Ministry from Kid Rock

The first song was "Born Free," the title song. As I listened, there are no words to describe the overwhelming awareness I felt of being in Kelly's presence. The words to that song were words like something Kelly would say. I believe with all my heart that God orchestrated it so that I would hear that song, on that day! I played the song at least twenty times. (As it turned out, the CD belonged to Kami. Cody told me Kelly had gone to a Kid Rock concert and was a huge fan.)

We had company, Dave Heigl, a speaker in to share at church, and I told Clifton and Dave about my experience when they got back home. I played the song for them. I loved how Kid Rock had sung about celebrating, "God's grace on me!"

I normally would not have listened to that CD, under any circumstance. For instance, from the time he was a young man, Kelly would bring me country music or other kinds of tapes and ask me to listen to this or that song; wanting to get my approval because it would mention the "man upstairs" or some other term referring to God.

When I found something that was rock music or what I deemed "not appropriate," I would sail his tapes across the pasture like a Frisbee. Kelly would protest and say they weren't his, and I always said, "Too bad!" Back then, I was a religious person and I didn't allow my kids to listen to anything but Christian music.

My theology has broadened, and my insights have grown deeper and wider in the things of God, grace and Heaven, especially since the passing of my son. Losing him has been an experience that I would've sworn I could not endure. When our friends lost their boys, I thought, "I could never endure that." We have three sets of great friends who've lost their boys, all of them before our own tragedy. I wondered, at the time, how they could continue with life.

Life Without Kelly

Frankly, after the reality set in on me that my son was gone forever from this earth, and that I wouldn't see him anymore – no more birthday calls, Mother's Day text messages – it was devastating. I was dead in the water.

I went back to work in hospice, I did my daily responsibilities, but I was so crushed over our great loss that I couldn't be who I wanted to be anymore. I tried to have joy, I tried to be "okay" for my husband and my family, but I was just numb. I experienced no real life at all – other than at church or when I was having my intimate time with the Lord. (That is still my favorite time, just me and the Lord; Him speaking to me; loving on me. There is nothing that compares to that oneness in God!)

Charlie and Jill LeBlanc were overseas when they heard about Kelly's tragic accident. They called immediately. They were going to be home on Thursday, and offered to come to our church on Sunday and conduct the service for us, and they said we didn't have to be there. They know the pain and loss of a son dying too early. We did go, and let their anointing pour over us, and afterwards they sat with us for hours and listened. They brought us loads of books, some that I'm just now opening. Those who have lost a child need to have plenty of time and space to grieve, and time to allow the healing power of God to wash over you.

October of 2011 was drawing near, and the closer it got to October 16th, the more I cried. I thought about having a memorial at the grave site, where we'd planned to bury Kelly's ashes, but Clifton said he couldn't do that. He was holding back, trying to make sure I was okay, and everyone else was going to be okay. Then, we started planning a memorial here in Missouri, a one year memorial, but we couldn't do that either. We didn't want to be anywhere without our son! So, I listen to my music, I listen to the Word of God. I sing, I read, I reach out to people who are hurting, and I've tried to accept the death of my precious son.

That's A Wrap!

In late 2010, David Hinton, the singing evangelist, had talked to us about a movie he had written, and asked us if Clifton and I would like to act in it. The movie script was based on a true story about his grandfather, who had worked in the moonshine stills of Tennessee at the turn of the last century, the early 1900's. Henry Walker was his name. Dave already had a song written about him called "How the West was Won." We were very excited to say, "Yes." David said he would call when he got the details together.

In March of 2011, David called us again and asked if we could come to Tulsa the first week of August for a cast meeting. At the meeting, we would go over the script, meet everybody and have a banquet. Clifton and I were so excited about this. The night of the meeting came – it was 113 degrees outside and we were meeting in a metal building with no air conditioning. The reason I mention it is because I saw the "supernatural-ness" of the movie that first night. People were excited, and they stayed in spite of the heat. I had not one dry stitch of clothing on after a couple hours. There were people at the meeting from all across the United States, and even a lady from England. Everyone had come at their own expense to be a part of a God-thing. We felt the anointing, and we knew something good was about to happen.

Honoring Our Son

David's son went after a swamp pump, which helped with the heat a little. David started the meeting with some music, then introduced us and called us up and had us share about how we were going forward since our son's tragic death. I think I shared that first night about how we felt the film was something we wanted to give our best to, so we could honor Kelly through the movie. We did the whole movie adventure under an anointing and a mandate to honor our son on the first anniversary of his too early death.

I can tell you Kelly would've been so proud of us, and I'm sure David would've found a place for him in the film, as Kelly was a true-blue cowboy, and looked majestic on a horse! David set us up afterwards with the Cooley's, a couple who always have a spare room ready for company. The room even had a bathroom, just like a hotel. (It was their ranch that we used for the movie.) The Cooley's had lost a daughter the year before, who was the same age as Kelly. Their daughter had had four children who the Cooley's were now raising. We all hit it off and had sweet fellowship.

One morning, the following month, David called us and said he was passing through Farmington, and could we have breakfast? We met Dave and his daughter, Rachel, in town and were happy to learn that he was planning to start filming our part of the movie on October 17. This would mean driving down to Tulsa on October 16th. What perfect timing!

Working on that movie was a huge blessing for me. No one in the film had any acting experience except Clifton and I, who were in our high school plays (as if that is something to brag about, after all, it was 50 years earlier). I remember the first scene we were in: David was in the corner writing furiously on a yellow notepad. I wondered about it at the time, but didn't ask him what he was doing. I thought maybe he was taking notes. Come to find out, David had written out the whole movie on paper, in longhand, and had kept it in his briefcase, but his briefcase was stolen in Texas a few weeks before the beginning of filming. So, Dave was actually writing out the movie, scene-by-scene, as we filmed. Who, but a genius, could do that?

Miracles for the Movie

One example of the many miraculous things that happened to pull off that movie is the way the props and settings were provided. The actual "town" you see in the film is storefronts only, with old buses behind the fronts. The saloon was built inside Dave's warehouse. We went to get costumes daily, and there were women who made outfits for us to wear. Clifton had an Amish friend make his leather vest, and he put the conchos on it. When Dave needed the moonshine still, he found one at a yard sale. The owner asked him what he was looking for, and he said, "I don't see what I need." The guy said, "Well, I have other things in the garage," so Dave said, "I need a copper whiskey still." This guy had one. He ended up selling it for half what he was asking. It may have been the same place where there was a big old safe, like you see in Western movies. Dave got it cheap, and it was full of valuable guns and other things. Movie material! And stuff to sell to finance the movie.

Dave was given horses, wagons – everything he needed. It was an exciting time. He plans to direct and produce a sequel. We've become forever friends with our 'co-stars' as a result of that film.

We were not without trials; there was much cause for pause, and at the time, no one would've blamed Dave for just forgetting the whole movie idea. But when a person has a vision and a call, God somehow gets them through and everyone is blessed for it.

Many of the extras in the film were folks who just happened on the set and we used them. One old feller, an elderly gentleman (he's dressed in western clothes in the movie), was just a customer at a feed store one day, and heard about the movie when someone from the film crew was there picking up a wagon part. This man got excited and brought his wagon over to the set the same day. So, he ended up driving his own wagon in the film, and in one scene I'm riding in it, on our way to the brush arbor meeting.

How the West Was Won is available on DVD and you can order one from us. Many souls have been saved as a result of that movie. We have carried it across the country, showing it and using the film as a ministry tool.

Relationships Restored

One place we took the movie was a Baptist church in our home town of Paoli, Indiana. On New Year's Eve 2011, Glenda Dowd-Tait, whom I'd met earlier that year, called us and gave us a word from the Lord. One of the things she said was that there would be restoration of relationships during the coming year. I knew it was true in my heart of hearts.

Something that had been building over the past three years, beginning with Ivan's death, was the rekindling of an old friendship with a couple from a Baptist church in Paoli. The man had been attending our family funerals, and he liked what Clifton was preaching. He told Clifton that he needed to get him into his church to share the message of God's unconditional love and grace. The meeting materialized in the fall of 2012, and we preached and played the movie in his church. We had three meetings full of the gospel of grace and wonderful fellowship, with many changed lives as a result.

Something awesome to note is the fact that we hadn't been around this couple for 35 years, not since we'd left the Baptist church in 1977. They wanted us to stay at their house. I was a little nervous, but I can tell you that from the moment we stepped out of the car, it was as if there'd never been a breach in our best-friend relationship. After all those years, we picked up right where we left off and had the most wonderful time imaginable. Now, whenever we return to Paoli, we get together if we can, and we've been back a couple of times to minister in their church. God is good!

Chapter 22

Cody: Drugs and Recovery

Cody has gone through a lot of tragedy with us. I'm making no excuses for him. However, I do understand how someone could turn to alcohol or drugs if they lack a real solid relationship with God. I can say for myself that I learned to trust God early on, but if I hadn't learned how to know Him intimately, I'm guessing that I too would've ended up trying to find another way to relieve the pain.

Cody has struggled with drugs for several years; he says seven years. In January of 2014, we thought he'd reached the bottom with the heroin addiction. Clifton brought him to our home, and we began a rehab regimen for him. He was 25 at the time, with no steady job, and no solid female relationship.

That January, I took him to a doctor who specialized in treating heroin addiction. After Cody got on the new medicine, he did well for a few months. Cody got a job he loved; he managed to have a relationship with a great girl – all with no drugs. It seemed we were all finally going to be okay.

We weren't. Cody and his nephew, Dustin Lee (Kelly and Darlene's eldest), had been using drugs off and on for a few years. Dustin went to prison soon after Kelly got killed. He's still there, but is scheduled for release in 2016. Dustin is a talented artist. He's had some opportunities to hone his skills, and he's excellent at what he does. We're hoping and believing for a new life for him and he is excited to get out of jail and start over. He had a scholarship to college before the drugs, and he had a Mennonite girlfriend and went to her church. His life was headed right. Then his dad left his family, causing everything to go "off." Dustin Lee's girlfriend wanted to see other guys at school, and Dustin had friends who were on pills that made them feel better, and that's how it started. Sad, very sad. Dustin Lee was raised in our church. He knows the Lord, and is a good person. He and Cody are like brothers. They were raised together until we moved to Colorado back when the boys were both seven years old.

Cody was arrested in 2012 and put in jail for distributing drugs. He got a five year probation with a ten year back up, meaning if he got another violation, he could go to prison for the full ten years. During the prior few months Cody was out of control, and no matter what we did to try to help, it only prolonged the inevitable.

My Heart is Broken

Drugs are from the pit of hell! People who are influenced by them are capable of anything. Cody has a raw, wicked, horrendous story to tell. He told me that as much as I know, I still don't know the worst.

All I really know is: Cody is our son, and I love him with everything in me – my whole heart and soul. But he has killed me dead on some issues. He took our debit card in the middle of the night, multiple times, and used it at an ATM, withdrawing all our money. I had our savings set up to sweep over to the checking account if for some reason we became overdrawn. All of that disappeared! He took our checks and ran them through at Wal-Mart, and so many bounced I had about a $1,000 in bad checks I had to cover, plus 600 dollars in overdraft charges. If we'd had him arrested, it would've added 25 years to his prison sentence. We were advised by our peers to do it, to have him arrested, but Clifton couldn't do it. I'd been down in Brazil on a mission's trip, and while I was gone it got worse – so bad that by the time I discovered the problem, we were drained and in a deep hole. Clifton didn't even have enough money for groceries while I was gone.

Cody took all of his musical equipment, computers and a camera, thousands of dollars' worth, and Clifton's family heirloom shotgun and went to the pawn shop (Clifton miraculously retrieved his shotgun). Clifton's tools were pawned. Cody took my old coins I'd collected since 1974: Kennedy half dollars; silver dollars; $100 in golden dollars still in their wrapping; some Buffalo Head nickels; many rare and uncirculated coins given to me by my mom. That was just the tip of the iceberg. It was painful to discover the truth.

One thing broke my heart so badly I couldn't even cry; there was not one tear. Cody emptied my DIME jar, which was full. An antique blue-green quart jar. Those dimes were my "Kelly Dimes." I was saving them to start a Kelly E. Coulter Foundation, an account set aside to give scholarships to kids so they could attend rodeo camps, or for other rodeo needs. Kelly had a heart for kids and he wanted to help them with anything that had to do with horses.

It's Worse than You Know

One day in the car, after he was clean, Cody tried to make amends for his actions. He told me, "Mom, it's worse than you even know." Cody proceeded to say that the first time he took dimes out of the jar, he took $20 worth. Cody took them to the bank to change into a twenty dollar bill. As he was getting out of the car, he said there was a twenty dollar bill in his path! Cody said he felt it was Kelly saying, "Here Cody. Here's twenty dollars, don't take Mom's dimes." Cody said, "I am such a worthless piece of $#!+. I took the twenty dollar bill *and* cashed in the dimes."

Cody did unspeakable things, and we were oblivious most of the time. However, after being deceived time after time, we began to wake up. I would go and buy Cody complete wardrobes, hundreds of dollars' worth of clothes and shoes he said he needed for jobs – jobs that never materialized. In the end, he would come back home with no clothes. Last year, when he came back home addicted to heroin, he had a Wal-Mart bag with only a few articles of clothing: a pair of underwear, a sock, and one T-shirt. He'd left a suit, shirt, dress shoes, socks, and all his jeans and shirts at a place where he'd been staying. The couple had moved away and we couldn't retrieve them.

So, when Cody came back to our home last year in January, we believed this time would be different. It was the day we had a snowstorm with below freezing temps, and the State Police had issued a warning to not be out in it. Dangerous temperatures. Clifton went to the barn to feed his animals, came back in, got the fire going in the fireplace, and said he wasn't moving the rest of the day. After a few minutes, Clifton suddenly said, "I have to find Cody!" He got into his 4x4 truck and disappeared into the blizzard. The Holy Spirit had prompted him to go, and led him right to Cody. Clifton found Cody – he was walking down the highway in tennis shoes, wearing only a sweatshirt and jeans. Cody had gone over to the church, taken a case full of Clifton's tools, and was headed towards the pawn shop. Drugs. That's what addicts do.

Clifton got Cody in the truck and took him to his apartment to get his clothes (the Wal-Mart bag) and brought him back to our home. He took Cody's girlfriend back to her parents' house.

Heroin at Applebee's

Later that month Clifton had to go out of town for ministry, so I took Cody with me to work. We felt we needed to be with him every moment. He wasn't yet on the medication that was supposed to stop the desire for heroin. On a Friday afternoon, I was finishing up my hospice visits; relieved that it was the weekend and that we were able to be on our way back to Farmington. Cody said he had a buddy who worked at Applebee's who was going to put in a good word for him to get a job. "Would I drive him there to put in his application?"

Well, we got to Applebee's on Friday about 6 p.m. I told Cody, "It's too crowded now. You need to come back in the morning." Cody insisted he had to go in right then. Later, I noticed that a 20 dollar bill was gone from my purse. Here's what happened:

I found out later that Cody had taken the money out of my purse and bought heroin at Applebee's!

That Sunday, I was ministering at the church in Clifton's absence. Cody was sick, and I'd left him home in bed. I was uneasy, but I had no choice and I came back home as soon as I could. Cody knew not to drive my Toyota - it had a water pump that needed to be replaced. Nevertheless, I came home from church to find that the Toyota was gone. Gone! Bad water pump and all.

I had "by mistake" left my phone at home and Cody was without a phone at the time. When I got inside, I found my phone in my room on the bed; not where I left it. I saw the numbers Cody had called, and I systematically called every one of them. Of course, no one had seen or talked to Cody. No one knew where he could be. I was frantic.

I drove everywhere I could think of, looking for Cody. Then I called the five numbers again. I said, "This is Cody's mother. If I do not hear from Cody within the next five minutes, you will have a policeman knocking at your door." Well, within three minutes, Cody was on the phone to me. I told him I was reporting the car stolen, and that he'd better have it back at the house immediately. I called the sheriff, and he met me at our house. The sheriff gave Cody a choice, "You can go to jail, or you can go to rehab at the hospital." Cody argued, he pleaded, he begged me, but I was done that day!

Breakdown

I was near a mental breakdown of some kind at this point. I can't even describe the kind of torment I was going through! I prayed constantly. I'd been prescribed a low dose of Xanax by my doctor when I went to see him in 2010 because I'd been crying about Kelly and couldn't seem to stop. Well, Cody began stealing all my Xanax, every month, before I could even get it out of the bag from the pharmacy. I kept refilling it so I would have a few, in case I needed them, but I never got to take them. Years' worth of medicine was stolen every month.

I hid the pills; I hid money. I had to hide our keys and I had to sleep with my purse. That period of time was a once-in-a-lifetime experience: never to be replayed again. However, hiding my things never worked. I had a gallon jar of change, mostly quarters that I was saving for the same purpose as the dimes, but they were taken too. Hundreds of dollars were in that jar. And, I had a smaller change jar I'd hidden under the bed – even placed stuff around it so it couldn't easily be seen by someone looking under the bed. All stolen! Nothing was ever safe.

Cody agreed to the ride to rehab to keep from going to jail and having the stolen vehicle charges filed. After he left in an ambulance, I felt like a ton of bricks had come off my shoulders! I was supposed to pick Clifton up at the airport in St. Louis that evening at six o'clock. I listened to praise music all the way, and tried to wash my mind and heart clear of the day's horror. I was thinking I would get Clifton in the car and we would stop somewhere and have a nice dinner and talk. I was so looking forward to a peaceful night and a good night's rest, but before we even got out of the airport, I received a call that Cody had left the hospital and was walking home. Oh my God of Heaven and Earth! No peaceful dinner, no peaceful sleep!

We Get Cody Some Help

Soon after this episode, we were able to get Cody to the doctor, get the prescription for an anti-heroin medicine, and Cody began rehab classes. He started to do well. After Cody had been on the medication and was in rehab for a while, he met someone who had a job at a sawmill, and he said Cody could work there. So Cody did, and he loved it and went every day. He got off drugs, was looking good and doing well. The church worship team loved him because he can play anything and would fill in on guitar, keyboard or drums. Cody added a dimension to the worship team that was anointed and wonderful.

The Girlfriend

He had a new girlfriend who was awesome, loved him and church, and she even got her parents coming to church. We liked her. She was cute and loving. However, for some reason, the old girlfriend (that we saw as poison to Cody) came back into his life. Everything went down from there, just as it had before. We finally had to tell him, "If you are going to be with her, we will not help you."

Now, I have to tell you, as grace people, we'd brought her to our home at one point given her a room, let them have a car to use to look for work, and supported them. Only to discover eventually that they were, both of them, still on drugs.

One night, they both had sprayed stuff up their noses on our porch. Clifton found out and got me up from a dead sleep at midnight (I was still working every day). We sat them down and gave them some new rules. She was asked to leave – to be gone the next day. They asked for one more day, at which time she drove off in our Lincoln (after snuffing some more spray up her nose) and totaled our car. It was an older car we rarely used and had only liability insurance, so the car was gone. We were called to come and pick up Cody (he wasn't with her when the accident happened). When we got to her parents' home, Cody told me we needed to buy her pain medicine, because her mom couldn't buy it. I told Cody, "Get into the car. We're going home." He refused. He ended up staying there.

This story is painful to write. I do know that God has kept Cody from dying – many times. We came to the conclusion that there is no way out of drugs, except God. We believed for his deliverance. The world will say only death or prison stops people from using drugs. When Cody went into rehab, the counselors told him he would always be an addict. He was clean then, and he told them he would not be a statistic.

So, this past fall, after we told Cody we weren't giving him any more money, we weren't giving him anymore use of the car, we weren't going to let him live with us if he was connected with his old girlfriend and he chose to leave. From then on, it was a fast, downhill spiral – a spiral that nearly caused the mental breakdown of both me and Clifton and some of our friends too.

Truly a Nightmare

On December 11, 2014, we were scheduled to leave for ministry in Kansas City. A few days before, Clifton said, "I don't see how we can go off and leave the house with Cody like he is." I knew we were in trouble, but we'd never canceled any meetings before because we were having problems, or for any other reason! Cody was mad at us. He was writing things on Facebook about us being terrible parents, "a$$holes" and that we wouldn't help him. He said he was homeless, cold, and hungry. I immediately called to cancel his phone and Facebook privileges, only to discover he'd just bought a new, expensive phone and that phone was under contract. I was told it would cost me $500 to cancel. However, I was able to suspend part of the plan.

Cody had been called in for an unscheduled probation meeting, so he'd come by the house to see if he could get cleaned up before he went to the meeting, and to tell us his girlfriend had been put into jail the day before. This was serious, and he knew it. Cody had violated his probation by not reporting a change of residence and for not paying fines, and he was scared. If his urine sample was dirty, he would have three counts against him, and he'd be a candidate for ten years in prison. Cody drove Clifton's truck to the probation meeting, which was near the jail. He failed his pee test and was sent to jail. The parole officer allowed him to drive the truck to the jail. We prayed mightily.

Cody called us on December 10 from jail. He told us he would've been dead if he hadn't been stopped. He considered it an act of God to be locked up in that awful place. We were relieved! We were so happy to know that his life had been spared as he could easily have died the night before from a drug overdose. There was now hope for a new beginning.

So we went to Kansas City and had a marvelous time. The ministry was anointed, people were saved and healed. We were able to celebrate a wonderful reunion with old friends, and we shared a little of our testimony with them and asked for prayer for Cody's deliverance.

Cody continues in the jail. He has a public defender who is younger than he is, but seems to be heartfelt in his passion for helping inmates. He likes Cody. He told me Cody has a lot on the ball, and that he's aware of his musical talents: he had heard Cody's band, the one he started before the drugs.

The plan is for Cody to get his time behind him. We tell him every week that he can do it. We could've bailed him out for a sum of money, but we believed God had said to leave him there. Recently, Cody was sentenced to a 120-day rehab program/addiction treatment in prison. Until then, he remains in the county jail, which is a privately owned hell hole.

I want to encourage mothers of drug addicts. Yes, there is hope. I am speaking from faith when I say that even though I know the hardest part is ahead of us, I have a peace and a conviction that Cody will preach the gospel, and be the evangelist he was prophesied to be. He is in agreement with that, and has always known he would do this. Even as a child, he told Clifton that we wouldn't have to change the initials on our ministry (CCM), because someday he would be taking over.

I also want to say this to mothers: Don't ever believe a word your child says while they're on drugs! Here are some signs of drug use: sleeping too much, staying up all night and days on end, not working steadily, always needing cash for something, things disappearing from your home. Also: weight loss, dark circles under their eyes and any negative changes in their physical appearance. It took me years to face up to the sobering truth that my baby son was a drug addict. He would swear "no drugs" and then accuse me of being crazy when I would act like I didn't believe him.

The Real Cody

The real Cody is an amazing person. Cody is generous, kind, funny, caring, anointed in ministry, musically talented, and gifted. This is the son we want to see emerge from recovery. This is the one God sees. In truth, God sees only this one, and has always only seen this one.

God loves all of us so much that He allows us to make our own choices. That is love – letting people do what they want to do. Cody says he believes it was a God-ordained act that he was placed in jail, and that he will follow God's plan now. Cody knows the power of the Holy Ghost, and he is ready to step out and warn young people to stay away from drugs, and to turn their lives over to a loving and caring God.

Chapter 23

My Mother

Dorothy June Redenbaugh was born on March 16, 1930 to Frederick Nathaniel and Edith Grace Weeks Redenbaugh. She was the fourth child of four and was brought up in a loving, country environment. Mom was popular in school – a cheerleader – beautiful with her black hair, green eyes and freckles. She had a lot of friends who love her to this day.

Mom got married when she was seventeen and my dad was sixteen years old. I can only imagine how difficult her situation must have been in 1947 as a senior in high school.

Pappaw Redenbaugh built an apartment for them onto their large home on Railroad Avenue in Paoli, Indiana. I lived there, and then two houses down, all of my life until I got married. Daddy paid my Pappaw five dollars a month for rent. When I was four years old, he was able to buy a home down the street. I remember the happiness in our home when that house was paid off (that would've been around the time I was in junior high school). I have two brothers, Monte Lee and James Edward. They're both smart, good lookin' and have been very successful in life – so successful, in fact, that they both retired early and enjoy life on their motorcycles and at the fishing hole.

I Loved Church

Mom tried to take me and my brothers to church. We attended a small country church south of Paoli called Apple's Chapel. There were, and still are today, a few small country churches around. I suppose they're named after the family who started the church.

I absolutely loved going to church. I felt a drawing there, and I enjoyed the other kids. I would practice gospel songs all week long with a neighbor, Joanie Hickman, and many Sundays we would sing a "special." Those memories are very dear to me. I received a few attendance pins for being there every Sunday for three months straight. Eventually though, my dad made it difficult for us to go to church, because he had fishing planned on Sundays, and he wanted to leave early. We only had one car, so everybody had to go to the same place. I don't remember any arguments about it, I only know that we stopped going to the little country church while I was still in grade school.

Go Now

I lost my mother on August, 2014. She was 84. I have regrets – we moved to Missouri eleven years ago. It seemed impossible to be back in Paoli for every birthday, every Christmas, and all the other holidays. I did the best I could (or thought I was doing my best) to be there as much as I could. However, the last Christmas Mom was alive, I was so tired from my too-busy life that I just didn't go. I felt justified in not going, because my family was represented. Darlene went and took three of her four boys and her fiancé (Her eldest son, Dustin Lee, was incarcerated, so he wasn't able to attend). The older I get and the more spread out our family becomes, the more I understand her heart in wanting us there with her. I remember thinking, "Next year I'll go." I admonish my readers to go now. We're not promised tomorrow. It's important to let those we love know it.

I've learned some things about my mom I didn't know. A few of her friends she kept in contact with have written to me. They miss her terribly. Mom was a good friend.

When Mom got sick, I went the extra mile or two to be there. I didn't think she would die. Not then. Mom was a strong woman, not sickly at all. She had diabetes, but watched her sugar and her diet, and didn't struggle with it. She had COPD from so many years of smoking even though she'd quit smoking years earlier, but it wasn't those things that were her demise.

Mom's best friend and common-law husband for twenty-five years was David Cox. He had a massive heart attack in January of 2013. Before that happened, he didn't want her to do certain things, like get out and walk. She did suffer with colds often, and for some reason, David thought he should take over with running the errands and even going to the mailbox. He was over-protective; I think that would be the appropriate term. David did the grocery shopping too. Mom hadn't driven her car for a long time. She had told me she was going to sell it. David had a truck and he took her wherever she needed to go. Mom was happy about that for the most part, and was so very glad he was there. She told me that she couldn't live in own her home if it wasn't for his help. I wondered about that, but I was never there long enough to see the whole picture.

After Dave's heart issues, Mom had to turn the tables and begin to do things, not only for herself, but also for Dave. I was so proud of her. She began to drive again, she went to the store and she was able to take Dave, with the help of my brothers, to the doctor and whatever needed to be done. I saw such intervention of the Lord we serve, getting her ready for the future. She had from January to November, when Dave passed away, to prepare to take care of herself.

"Oh, Could You?"

In September 2013, Mom called me and was crying over Dave's condition. Not classic Mom, so I knew I needed to go to Paoli. I said, "I'll come there and sit with you, take you back and forth, or whatever you need." Dave had been placed in the nursing home for some rehab after more heart issues, kidney and lung problems. I expected Mom to say, "No, you don't need to come," but instead she said, "Oh, could you?" So I went home, got things in order to go, and left the next morning.

Mom had gone from not even getting dressed in the mornings to getting up early, getting ready to go to the nursing home, driving out there, and staying with David until he went to bed. Then she drove home in the dark, went to bed, and started the same thing all over the next day. She did this for the entire three months he was there. I enjoyed my time that week with Mom and my brothers. And Dave – he was something else!

Dave had come to one of our evangelistic meetings and had raised his hand to get saved. Clifton prayed with him, and we knew he was born again. So many times, when someone doesn't become involved with a church, a bible study, or even their own study, the enemy of our souls tries to convince that person that God isn't pleased and then the individual's mind gets condemned.

In the nursing home, Dave developed a condition called C. difficile, or C. diff. It's an infection of the bowels and digestive system and it's very contagious and common in hospitals and nursing homes. A major symptom of C. diff. is diarrhea and digestive tract pain. In my hospice work I'd heard of it often, but in my experience, it's easily treated with antibiotics. I'd never heard of anyone dying from it (although I know now that people do die from it). Everyone going in to see Dave was supposed to wear gloves and gowns but, of course, Mom refused to wear them. She could be stubborn and that was a "pass down" from her mother! (I'm told it skipped me entirely. Smile.)

Sadly, the week Dave was supposed to come home after having pneumonia, he passed away. Mom had just arrived home from being with him when she received a call from the facility. A heart attack was the cause of death. My brothers and I wondered how Mom would do. She was very sad, and missed Dave terribly. I talked to her on the phone a couple times a week. She was having pain in her abdomen, and her doctor thought it was her gall bladder.

At one point, being the strong, positive woman she was, she told me, "I am going to get a new car (which she did) and I am going to start going to the senior citizen's dances and dinners." Monte, Jimmy, and I thought, "Go Mom!" She'd been good at reinventing herself in the past, and it looked like she was going to do it again. However, as the months progressed, her health deteriorated. A test for C. diff. fell through the cracks, even though she'd gone to the doctor, and talked with the doctor's office on the phone many times.

C. Diff.

Finally a test was done in June and she was sent to the Bloomington hospital. She was treated, but never felt comfortable about going back home. She knew she wasn't over the C. diff; she didn't feel she was ready to go home, but for some reason (perhaps it was insurance) she was shipped out of there. She never did recuperate.

In July, Clifton and I had to be in Indiana because his nephew passed away, and we were needed to do the funeral and be with family. Mom was still sick. Clifton had to go back home, but I stayed behind to be with Mom. By this time, she couldn't eat anything, had lost about 60 pounds, and looked terrible. Everyone thought it was grief. We'd gone to a restaurant with my son and she couldn't even order something to eat. I took her to the doctor. They did a test on her gall bladder, but they said that wasn't the problem. She had no relief from anything she'd tried. Her doctor ordered her a high-powered antibiotic and she was going to start on that.

Towards the end of July, I needed to go see Clifton's sister, who'd lost her son to cancer. I made sure Mom had everything she needed, and that she felt at ease with me being gone for an hour. I got her settled in her chair, left her with her portable phone, her cell phone, a glass of water, and a protein drink she was sipping on. I was hurrying because I didn't want to leave her there alone for very long. When I got back, she was lying face down on the concrete fieldstone patio, and she couldn't get up! Her phones were still on the porch. She had a goose egg lump on her head, her nose was scraped and bleeding, and her wrist and elbow were cut. She was so weak she couldn't manage to get up on her own.

I finally got her up and back into the chair and got her cleaned up. She said she'd wanted to water her flowers. Mom! We decided there was nothing broken and that she didn't need to call 911. That was Saturday night. She had an appointment on Monday to go to the doctor. I took her in and spoke with the doctor privately and asked him to insist she go into rehab to strengthen her legs. He consented and Mom went along with the plan. Reluctantly.

I couldn't go home without knowing she was being taken care of, but my brothers stepped in to look after things. I left, and Mom was in the rehab for a while, but she didn't do well in there. She just couldn't rally and get better.

Finally, after she was sent to the hospital for pneumonia, they discovered that she had the C. diff virus. She went from the hospital in Paoli to Bloomington hospital. Her C. diff count was so high a nurse told me she'd never seen a count that high. By this time, Mom was in so much pain, she was bloated and couldn't eat or void through her bowels.

At the time, my brothers and I were trying to believe those doctors were going to help our mother. If we had to do it over again, we'd definitely do some things very differently. (Wouldn't we all?)

There was a hospitalist on staff who told us most assuredly that they could turn Mom around, and that she would be fine. Mom was assigned an internist, a lung doctor, a heart doctor, a kidney doctor, a specialist for swallowing, and on and on it went. I could say what I really think, but that wouldn't benefit anyone.

Going Home

Suffice it to say, after a while it got to the point where Mom wanted to go home. She knew she was dying. I couldn't receive it. I knew it in my heart, but not in my head. After working in hospice for six years, I still couldn't believe it was happening; I kept praying and believing Mom could have a few more good years in her home, if she could just come out of her present condition. I thank God for a doctor who came in her room one day and said, "Why does she have this?" It was a small bag of clear liquid being pumped into her veins, and we'd been told it cost $10,000 per bag. He was clearly angry. He asked to speak to us, and finally told us the truth. Before this, we kept thinking she could get better. He told us she needed to be unhooked from all IV's except the pain medicine, and that it was time for her to go to Hospice House.

I asked, "Could I please just take her home?" Mom had told me, "I just wanna go home, sit on my porch and watch my hummingbirds." The doctor said she couldn't make the fifty mile trip home. My brothers worried about me being able to take care of her, but Mandy, a family member who is a CNA (Certified Nursing Assistant) told me she would help me, and that we could do it. The doctor said if we took her to Hospice House for a few days and she stabilized, then I could bring her home. I was in such denial, I believed him.

So, with all of us kids in agreement, the ambulance took her to Hospice House. She was placed in room number 8. Yes, Room 8 (remember, eight is God's number for New Beginnings). Her view was a whole wall of glass that looked out into the woods and nature. Beautiful. I doubt if she saw it. My son Dustin came to see his Mammaw. He and Mandy talked with her. She knew him, and told him she loved him. That was about 6 p.m. on the 18th of August. That is the last thing she said. She closed her eyes for the last time. The boys and their wives left. I made a bed on the couch, and still didn't believe she would pass before I could take her back home.

I held her hand and about eight o'clock I asked her to squeeze my hand if she could hear me. She didn't. I talked to her anyway, believing she could still hear me, even though there was no sign she could. I lay down, believing I would talk to her the next morning. On August 19th, I awoke to the nurse announcing she was going to bathe Mom. I got up and stood there beside the bed, and the nurse said, "Geri, you should call your brothers. Your mother is making some changes."

Her fingernails were blue. Mom took a couple more breaths and was gone. I was shocked; I think she had waited for me to wake up and come stand by her side.

Precious Memories

My mother. A flood of memories, like the song, "Precious Memories," began to overwhelm me. My thoughts went back to when I was growing up, and then bounced back to the present. I do know that my mother loved me very much, but neither Mom or Dad were "loving," as in hugs, kisses, or even encouraging words. Nobody ever said, "I love you." I suppose I lived in a dream world of sorts. I remember thinking, as I was growing up around my relatives, that I was a very lucky girl, because I did feel very special around them. My dad's sisters and my cousins were awesome to me, and I spent a lot of time with them growing up. Mom's family were great people too, funny and adoring to all of us.

My favorite times were the holidays at my Mammaw Redenbaugh's house. My Granny Grimes was different from my other grandmother, but I loved and cherished them both. Later, they were both interested in my radio program, and came to my church as often as they could. They loved me and I felt it; knew it! God was so very good to me, even before I knew Him.

We had a beautiful memorial for her, a celebration of life service. I wrote this poem to read at the service:

Our Mother

Mom was an artist, a quilter, a jewelry maker.

She crocheted, she created; was a great cook and baker.

An author, too – she knew how to write.

Her letters were long, newsy and filled with delight.

Family history was a passion for her, and there are many books

of love

Containing facts she gathered for years, with help from above.

Mom was called a "rare jewel," a "blessing and joy" this

week in a card from a friend.

Mom never got to read it though, sadly, she had already come

to the end.

But I know she knows and smiles.

The card came from many miles away.

Mom's friendship was cherished by no, not a few:

There is Helen, Martha Jean, and Libby, true blue.

There are others, and family who knew she'd be "there."

She was faithful, honest, and someone who cared.

Mom kept her word; a Virtuous Woman was she,

With strength and honor as her clothing, and always will be.

Our Mother left a memorable footprint on this earth she trod.

Now forever she'll rest High on the Mountain with God.

I went to her house after the funeral, and sat in her chair day after day. There was no cell phone service, so I had a lot of quiet time. I read some of her journals, prayed a lot, and thought about her. We'd had some good talks in the hospital, and at her house, before she went to the hospital. My Mom planted a lot of good seed in me. I'm like her in so many ways. My mother made the best out of her situations. She stuck with my dad through thick and thin. He was not easy to live with.

Mom thought I worked too hard, and her voice still calls out, "Geri Anne, you are going to have to slow down." She was right. I told her I didn't know how, and she said, "Well, no one can change that but you."

I took a leave of absence from hospice to be with her, to recover from the summer, and to take care of Mom's "after death" business. When I returned in the fall to my hospice chaplain position, I was told I wasn't needed anymore; what an answer to prayer! Honestly, I wasn't ready to go back. Mom would have been very proud of me taking it easy a little bit, and thanks to the inheritance she left me, I'm not stressed about finances. I thank her every day. Those finances were a restoration of all Cody took, and more. God is so awesome!

I found a letter she'd written to me when I was telling her I couldn't come to Indiana. I was surprised. I didn't remember receiving such a letter. In the letter, she told me she understood that my time wasn't my own, and that I had a call from God I needed to fulfill. We wrote letters back and forth; for years she preferred that means of communication. Finally, after cell phones came along and we were able to talk anywhere, anytime, I got her to switch from writing to calling. However, for most of my time away, she wrote me a letter at least once a week, and I have a mountain of them. I never threw any away. I miss Mom's updates on family and friends. She was my connection to many family members I haven't heard from since her death.

Sounds from Heaven

Something happened the day I was set to leave Mom's (I'd stayed for two weeks after the funeral). I was leaving before daylight on a Sunday morning because I had been scheduled since last January to speak at a new place, a Methodist church in Illinois. I'd thought about canceling, but sitting in Mom's recliner one evening, God poured a message into me just for them, so I kept the engagement.

The car was packed. As I closed the back door to her house, I paused and stood in the doorway for a moment. The air was dead still, no breeze. It was already very hot. I looked over at her huge flower garden, which she had loved so much, and began to weep. Through some big tears, I told her how very sorry I was that I hadn't been able to bring her back home so she could watch her hummingbirds one more time.

Suddenly, without warning, there was the faint sound of one her porch chimes tinkling, ringing – except there was no breeze! I knew then. Mom was letting me know it was okay. She was just fine with things. And very happy.

Since Mom's passing, I find shiny pennies several times a week. She would tell me when I was a kid, "Now, when you find a penny, that means to trust God, because it says on there, "IN GOD WE TRUST."

Chapter 24

Heaven

Many years before Kelly went to Heaven (back in the 1980's in fact), I received insights about Heaven while I was studying the book of Revelation and getting ready to preach. Then years later, while I was vacationing in Branson in 2006, I saw a presentation about Heaven done by a woman dressed all in white. She seemed very peculiar but she stole my heart away with her scriptural description of Heaven and what she said lined up perfectly with the revelation I'd received years earlier.

John the Apostle said he was *"in the Spirit on the Lord's Day"* (Revelation 1:10) and from then on has an outrageous story. He was alive during the Church Age, the same dispensation of time that we're living in today. When I got to Revelation chapter 21, I began to see things I sensed the church needed to know – even the whole world – so I've been teaching those things all across America and around the world ever since.

Heaven Is Real

I've encountered many people over my lifetime in all the various places we've lived and traveled, both ministers and "lay folks" alike, and I've found that the average person walking the streets today has no clear, scriptural idea about Heaven. They don't know what it's like or even if it actually exists. To the average believer, Heaven is viewed as a place of mystery, filled with vapor, clouds, lights, and spirits. Angels hover around the throne; there are gold streets, jewels and a bright light.

However, as I began to study Revelation, Chapter 21, a different picture became clear. Heaven is actually the New Jerusalem. John saw a city coming down from Heaven, from God, and he said he heard a loud voice from Heaven saying:

"Behold the tabernacle of God is with men, and He will dwell with them, and they shall be His people, and God Himself will be with them, and be their God." (Revelation 21:3)

I am convinced that this is the New Heaven. Heaven is where God dwells, the city God will set on the New Earth - this earth – only brand new. The heavenly city has streets of gold, the walls of jasper, the jewels, the glitz and the glitter! It's the NEW HEAVEN, where the throne of God is, where His presence is. Heaven is a city that sets on the New Earth and it will be the most beautiful place we could ever imagine.

I came to a stunning conclusion after studying various near-death experiences. (I had to sit up and take notice!) I've read reports and heard testimonials from folks spanning three centuries and everyone shares the same story, even though they've never spoken to each other or met personally. For instance, Rebecca Ruter Springer, a woman who had a near-death experience in 1860, tells some of the same stories as Don Piper did in his 2004 book, "90 Minutes in Heaven." That isn't a coincidence.

There is a thread that runs through the Bible that teaches us about the nature of God, which is love. From those witnesses who've experienced the grand and glorious place we call Heaven, we can see the love of God; the fullness of Him.

In Heaven, we will be more alive than we've ever been before. My son and my mother are more alive today than when they were on Earth. Heaven is a real place, not a spiritual mystery or myth. I used to think Heaven was just a spiritual "state." I didn't understand how tangible it is in every way. Heaven is huge, bigger than we can comprehend. For example, everything on Earth is a copy – just a type or shadow of things already in Heaven. You can read in Exodus and other Old Testament books how God gave instructions to folks to build things here on Earth from a pattern they saw in Heaven. Heaven is the blueprint!

Every Good Thing

Anything and everything you ever wanted to do, you'll be able to do in Heaven. God will fulfill your every heart's desire, wildest dreams and expectations. I believe, for example, that if you ever wanted to play the piano while you were on Earth, well, in Heaven you'll take a lesson or two (maybe you won't even need lessons) and sit down at the grandest piano you ever saw and play anything your heart desires. People will come to hear you and your talent will be a gift to them. Worship will flow freely; no inhibitions. If you're an artist or ever desired to be one in your earthly life, in Heaven you will paint, draw, sculpt, and give away masterpieces as gifts to those you love.

Our gifts are without repentance (see Romans 11:29). Our enjoyment in doing things like swimming, horseback riding, skate boarding, football playing, fishing, hunting, – WHATEVER –will only be intensified in our eternal home. I believe we'll have only the best Heaven has to offer and that our joy will be unspeakable and full of glory!

"How do you know this, Sister Geri?" That's a good question. I know my Father! I've read the Bible and I have received the revelation of His deep love for us. The disciple John wrote in his gospel about God's unsearchable love (see John 17:23). There isn't enough room on earth to hold the books that could be written about the things Jesus did and said while He lived here. He was good, and had only our good on His mind.

There is more written on Heaven in the Bible than we've noticed. When we see something in the spirit, then we see it every time we open our Bibles. That's how it is with me and Heaven. I see it everywhere, and I believe God has hidden some things through the ages for such a time as this. Daniel, who wrote the book in the Bible bearing his name, revealed many prophetic events. There came a time, mentioned in Daniel 12, when Daniel was told to close the book. Well, I believe that book is opening again, and I believe there is much more for us to experience with our God while we live and breathe right here on planet Earth.

Heaven is Awe-some!

Every person I've ever read about who has come back from Heaven reports that music vibrates out of the flowers, the sidewalks, the animals, even the water. All kinds of music too, not just hymns from the old days. Heaven has an appeal to every age and every nationality. Aborted and miscarried babies are there. God will have them waiting for us when we arrive. I have, waiting for me: a miscarried baby, a miscarried grandchild, and a stillborn granddaughter, Kelsey JoyAnne. Our relatives are caring for them until we "mamas" arrive.

We will not miss one thing we had on Earth. I heard someone once say that those who go to Heaven early will not miss anything they might've wanted to see on earth, such as a child growing up. I've grieved over Kelly missing so much life with his boys, but over time I've developed a peace that God is God, nothing is impossible with Him, and that He will make right all that was wrong. We have a GOD! And our God is alive and can and will do anything! We could ask, "How is this possible?" I just gave you the answer! He is a God of restoration. In fact, there will be a great restoration even before we all go to Heaven. Acts 3:21, speaking of Jesus, says, *"Whom heaven must receive until the times of restoration **of all things**, which God has spoken by the prophets since the world began."* (emphasis mine)

The Apostle Paul said he went to the *"third heaven"* and he didn't know if he was in his body or out of his body (see 2

Corinthians 12:2). Enoch and Elijah went to Heaven as mortals. Elijah and Moses were transfigured on the mountain, and they spoke with Jesus there. My point is, in Heaven we are real people, living in real homes and have real lives.

Mansions

I've also heard many testimonies about our rooms in Heaven. The word "mansions" in John 14 is the Greek word "rooms" (my daughter had a dream about Kelly after he went to Heaven, and he told her he wanted to bring her to Heaven to see his room).   In our room will be everything we could imagine (and much we can't comprehend) that will bring us joy. I'm fully persuaded that there will be everything we have ever desired in our room. I believe with every fiber of my being that all we care about is awaiting our arrival there because the rooms John spoke of are built specifically for each individual, containing every beautiful color and fabric (they will be beyond our imagination or comprehension). They will be colors, fabrics, and styles designed just for us!

My room will have lots of roses, daisies, old fashioned quilts and embroidery, books and a beautiful desk with paper, pens and all kinds of greeting cards. Music will be playing continually and, oh yes; my room will have dishes, lots of dishes. (And I'll be the one who learns to play the piano.)

I've listened to countless CDs and read a large collection of books on the subject of Heaven. A few things stuck as revelation, things I knew to be truth because my spirit bore witness. A recommended reading list can be found in the Appendix at the back of this book.

There is a place in Heaven where we'll all meet together and enjoy sweet fellowship. We will live next to family and friends and we'll eat together and delight in our new life. My family will have a wonderful ranch full of the best horses, the most beautiful barn ever built, with cows and chickens too. Our favorite pets will be there. My middle son, Dustin, and my grandsons, Brady, Bracey, and Jaden are golfers, and they'll have a supreme course. Athletes will have the best available fields and equipment and no one will ever get dirty, mad or hurt.

The Meal in Heaven

Another revelation came to me a few years ago. I was compelled to go to a meeting that I didn't want to attend. I felt I didn't have time because I was working full-time with hospice and my weekends were needed to rest my head. But, my friend Gwen Shields invited me, and I had told her I would come to her meeting. So, on Friday after work, I drove to the boondocks, to a lodge on a lake out in the middle of nowhere, west of St Louis. I have a lesson here: just because we don't want to do something does not mean we shouldn't do it. I'm a woman of integrity, and I keep my word "to my own hurt." That is one reason why I consider myself a success. Sacrifice for others is a huge brownie point with God. Now, don't go thinking I did it to gain a brownie point. No. However, after following the Holy Ghost for forty-five years, I've noticed that when I listen to Him and am obedient, whether I'm happy about it or not, He always, without fail, blesses me out of my socks, and does something awesome. I wasn't thinking along those lines at all though, I was just going because I said I would, complaining the whole way. I even got lost and had to be rescued.

BUT THEN...Mary Dorian began to speak that first night. She was speaking about Heaven, dreams, and other prophetic insights. In her message, she nonchalantly mentioned that Moses, Aaron, Nadab, Abihu, and 70 elders had had a meal with God on a mountain. I thought "What?!" For the first time in my life, I raised my hand in the meeting and asked, "Where is that scripture?" Mary was so confident; she just waved her hand and said, "Oh, I don't know, I will find it for you later."

As the meeting progressed, I was completely blessed and received much revelation. I forgot all about the scripture. Later, when we talked during a break, I told my "dime story." A couple of the ladies who were sitting there with us got up to go to the restroom, and came back shouting, holding up a dime! Yes, it was lying on the floor in the corner of the restroom.

When I got home, I was talking to my husband about what Mary had said about Moses eating a meal on the mountain, and Clifton had never heard of such a thing either, even though we've both read the Bible through several times. I was sitting on the couch. I grabbed my Bible, and it fell open to Exodus 24. My eyes fell upon the very scriptures Mary had spoken of to us! Is that amazing? Here is the scripture from Exodus 24:9-11: *Then Moses went up, also Aaron, Nadab, and Abihu, and seventy of the elders of Israel, and they saw the God of Israel. And there was under His feet as it were a paved work of sapphire stone, and it was like the very heavens in its clarity.*

But on the nobles of the children of Israel He did not lay His hand. So they saw God, and they ate and drank.

Are you still on your feet? Because I was blown away; flabbergasted, and absolutely in a state of wonderment and amazement.

Jack Hayford's comment in his Spirit-Filled Bible says, "He did not lay His hand" meaning they "survived the ordained, intimate experience." After all, the Word does say no one has seen God and lived! I believe when the Bible says, *"As it were, a paved work of sapphire,"* it's telling us there are no words to explain the substance they saw. I believe Heaven came down for those elders. Either that or they were taken up to Heaven for a meal with God. I meditated for many weeks and months on that passage of scripture. It holds power for me that I'm unable to articulate. I began to ask people, especially preachers I've known all my ministry life, many of whom have been preachers much longer than me, if they knew about that scripture. None of those I asked had ever heard of it.

Then, one weekend in 2014, I was going to Indiana to see my Mom and have a birthday celebration with my son and grandsons who have birthdays in April. My friend, Marci Calloway, who I've known for over thirty years, called me one Thursday. We're friends, and we've talked periodically over the years, but I hadn't seen her since we moved to Missouri ten years before that. She said to me, "Geri, next time you come to Indiana, why don't you come and spend the night with me?" I was leaving the next morning, so I said, "I'm coming tomorrow. I can come straight to your house because I'm not due to see my family till Saturday." She was excited, so I went.

It's difficult to explain, but that meeting was another God-ordained (following the Holy Spirit) moment. From the time I arrived, I knew something was different. Marci was on my page with some Hebrew language and calendar events that I'd been studying, and we talked non-stop, long into the night.

When I saw how deep she was into some things I'd only surfaced, I asked her, "Do you know about Moses and the elders eating and drinking with God?" Yes, she knew, and went directly to Exodus 24! I knew God had reunited us for a reason. We had been close since we'd both come out of legalism in the mid 90's, but with the move to Missouri and all, we hadn't been together in a long time, although we'd always prayed for each other.

I realize what I am saying about Heaven is a lot to take in if you've never sat down and thought about it. When my grandparents passed, I was a believer, but I knew nothing about Heaven. I was one of those who envisioned Heaven to be just a place in the spirit, a mystery. The scripture I quoted from Acts 3 has significant meaning regarding our heavenly experience and the tie between Heaven and Earth. Angels have come in this age and spoken to people who were open and listening. People living today have had encounters with angels. Angels have saved my life many times, but I've never seen one. They are ministering spirits. Hebrews 1:14 says: *Are they not all ministering spirits sent forth to minister for those who will inherit salvation?*

"*Those who will inherit salvation*" is speaking about you and me. How exciting!

I would highly recommend you get some books on Heaven. I can say the ones I've recommended (see Appendix) are excellent. I believe knowledge about Heaven is an evangelistic tool and it brings comfort to those who have loved ones who've gone on. I have been greatly comforted by the things God has shown me, and by the testimonies of people who have "been there." We have a hope and a future, and we'll pass on through, leaving our body (our "earth suit") behind, but our soul and the spirit will live on forever. When we arrive at Heaven's gates we will finally be made complete!

Chapter 25

On Being a Pastor's Wife, Mother and Friend

I have a deep admiration for pastor's wives. No one really knows, except us, what we endure to serve people. The Lord spoke to me, before I even knew how to hear Him very well, and told me that He was calling me to be a "preacher's wife." I love my calling from God. He has blessed me far beyond what I could ever comprehend well enough to speak in words. I would do it all over again. Well, almost all.

In the beginning, in 1977, I had no idea what was going to happen. All I knew was I had answered a call from the One who loved me more than anything I'd ever experienced. My biggest challenge has always been to stay soft and pliable, forgiving and understanding. I've learned, over the years, to put myself in other people's shoes, and to try to see things from their perspective. I'm not saying I'm always right, but I'm right a lot! Smile.

It's all because I have a relationship with the Holy Spirit. I do hear Him. I know Him well. He tells me things to come, like the Bible says. My problem is, I tell others what they need to do, and it isn't always accepted. When I preach from the pulpit, I'm sharing what I believe, with all my heart, to be true and relevant to all of our lives. It is painful when my words, which are anointed by the Spirit of the living God, are ignored and treated as if they don't matter.

On the other hand, I love it when people come back to me and say, "Geri, I started doing what you said, and my whole life has changed!" As pastors, we're called to edify, to instruct, to train, and to build up the body of Christ. We tell those, who we are shepherds over, everything we know in order to help them become victorious, prosperous and healthy. When someone is receptive, it makes all the pain we go through worth it.

A Preacher's Wife

Pastors – those truly called and serving out of a heart of love and respect for God – are blessed above measure. There are some that start out right, with a pure heart to help people, but then they go way off like Jim Jones in the 70's. Clifton was called a Jim Jones one time because of the faith message we were preaching. I'll never forget what Clifton said: "Are you serious? I can't even get people to come to church, never mind drink poison!"

I've seen loving, dedicated pastors be so mistreated, so beat up, so discouraged, and so disappointed in people and themselves that they quit and ran for the hills. I know one couple who gave and gave, laid down their lives for the good of their people, and were ultimately cut open and put through a meat grinder so intense that they ended up moving as far away from people as they could. They actually ended up living in the woods, on top of a mountain, in a home with no electricity or running water; all just to be away from people. That's the most extreme case I'm aware of, but we knew them well, loved them, and still do. We know others who've left the ministry to sell cars or insurance. The pressure of ministry takes a toll on the entire family.

Somehow, we always knew God had called us and had a plan for us. In my heart, I've gone back many times to the night Clifton answered the call to preach. It was miraculous, powerful, and I knew it was real. So, just when I think I can't do it anymore, God always shows up in a big way. Sometimes it's just that still, small voice, but He always speaks to me and when He does, I'm good to go!

I've seen and experienced being lied about, being the object of someone's demonic jealousy, and suffering betrayal of such magnitude that, sometimes, it's difficult to ever trust anyone ever again. I know what it's like to give it ALL – every dime – to keep the church going, and still see failure. We've emptied savings accounts, kid's piggy banks; looked for change under the sofa cushions, and used every cent to find enough gas money to get somewhere to preach. Sometimes we just took off with no gas, believing God was sending us somewhere and that He would fill the gas tank along the way. And we never ran out.

A pastor's wife sacrifices her own happiness to fulfill the call of God. I do believe that God wants us to be happy, and I know He has rewards for all of us who are obedient, but there have been times when I've asked God, "Do I have to keep doing this?" The folks that you love and serve and would do anything for, they are the very same folks who will just walk right out the church door next week, without a word, taking their fan club with them.

To be completely fair, I would also like to address those who have been crushed by a pastor or church leadership. This goes both ways, as I mentioned earlier in the book. We were loyal and faithful to our church. I have experienced, and heard horror stories about the faithful saints who have suffered at the hands of church leadership and their failings. It ought not to be this way! Even though Clifton and I have been passionate about being the best pastors possible, we have also hurt people, unknowingly, and caused folks to leave the church. As pastors we all must operate in God's Grace and His unfailing love. It breaks my heart to hear these stories about why the saints do not go and support a local assembly. I believe God's heart is expressed in the Gospel of John Chapter 17. I read this in a small group meeting recently: *That they all may be one, as you Father are in me, and I in you that they may be one in us, that the world may believe that you have sent me.* (John 17:21)

Overall, I've been so blessed, I can hardly contain it. I've had a great "pastor's wife" life! The incredible moments when I've seen people's lives changed forever far outweigh the lonely, difficult times. We have traveled across the United States, from shore to shore, preaching and teaching the Word of God. We've also been in many other nations, at their invitation, sharing our knowledge and revelation of God's love.

Being a Mom in Ministry

Being a mom AND a preacher's wife has been a joy for my family and also a deep wound for me and my kids. After coming into grace, the situation got better. I believe our congregation has accepted us for who we are. Flawed, yet called. We have problems just like other families. Thankfully, the group we pastor now has been a life saver and a great encouragement to us and our family. They've walked through the valley of the shadow of death with us, and supported us through thick and thin. They've remained faithful through the era of Cody's drug addiction, and the awful things he did during that time. They also stood with us through Kelly's death. We have the best people ever!

Looking back is both painful and extremely joyful for me. When we lived and pastored in Indiana, our family always attended the churches we led. By family, I mean everyone: all our children, all the spouses, the grandkids. Everybody knew that on Sundays there were no other plans made but to be sitting there, in church, listening to their Dad and Pappaw. We ate together a lot and those were precious, memorable times, branded on my heart forever. Now some of the kids are grown, and we're too spread out to all be together very often. Life goes on, and we've had to adjust to change.

Priorities

Everything changed for me when Kelly died, Cody got on drugs, Dustin Lee went to prison, and the church had difficulties. Yes, my joy is in the Lord and I have kept the joy of the Lord, but would I go back and change anything? Yes, I would! The ones in the congregation who I sacrificed for, they later left me hanging out to dry; but my kids were always there after the smoke cleared. My family has come to mean the whole world to me, and I learned that I'll be there for them no matter what.

At the end of the day, your family is there for you. They won't go anywhere. My one, deep regret is that I put the church people ahead of my family to a fault. I didn't realize it at the time, and I did make sure the kids had what they needed, but I have regrets. I admonish women in ministry to remember to keep your priorities straight.

I love my kids beyond what they will ever know. I tried to apologize to Kelly one time for raising him the way we did. We had no money, and we were strict on the kids as far as rules went. Kelly told me, "Mom, I'm glad you raised me like you did, and I wouldn't change a thing." I'm not sure what the other three kids would say about their upbringing, except that we were strict on them, and legalistic to a fault. They do know the power of God, and that He's real and loves them and will help them. Maybe I did do something right. Their Dad has a lot to do with their faith. He's their hero and favorite preacher ever!

I desire to be a mom whose kids will say, "She loved me." That's enough.

On Being a Friend

It is my nature to be a loyal friend. If you have me for a friend, I will defend you. I will stick by you, I will pray for you, and always believe God's best for you (see Proverbs 18:24). As far as I know, I've never dumped anyone as a friend, but I've certainly been dumped a time or two.

I have "pastor's wife" friends, ministry friends, and casual acquaintances that I believe will become my friends in the future. My ministerial friends are so precious to me. I can't say it eloquently enough! We've spent our entire ministry career building those relationships and I have a desire to plant into them, to sow, to love and to let them know how valuable they are to me.

Some women say to me they have no friends. My thoughts are, "Are you showing yourself friendly?" It takes sacrifice to have friends. Reach out. Sow into other ladies' lives. You will reap what you sow.

Be Careful What You Ask For

Once I had a good friend, who I thought loved me, but wasn't behaving normally towards me. So one day I asked her if I had offended her in some way. She exploded on me with a long list of offenses. Apparently, I had unknowingly projected a lot of unpleasantness towards her. I was shocked at her reply. In fact, it was one of the biggest shocks ever.

Be careful what you ask for. This was just a few days before my Annual Harvest Time Ladies' Conference (perfect timing for the enemy to attack me). I left there bawling uncontrollably. I felt like I never wanted to minister again.

On my way home, I noticed a voicemail on my phone, so I listened to it. I heard a friend saying, "Oh Geri, I can't wait to get under your anointed teaching this weekend, and I'm bringing a carload of ladies with me!"

When I got home, there were four letters in my mailbox. Each one thanked Clifton and me for our ministry to them over the years, and testified to us how we had changed their lives. They sent a total of $1500 in love offerings!

Then to top it off, God sent me a new friend, Karen Carr, who I met in Wal-Mart. We immediately connected, and she has been a good, faithful friend for over three years. We've traveled together, ministered together, and we pray for each other. She is someone I can call to go to lunch and we have fun. God's faithfulness overwhelms me!

Sisterhood

I want to mention a set of friends who are a breath of fresh air to me, a unique and valuable sisterhood. I graduated high school in 1966. My high school girlfriends and I were very close during school and loved each other to the moon! Over the years, as we were raising our families, we would see each other occasionally, and even plan a Christmas gathering or a summer reunion at one of our homes. Then, one time Brenda Weeks Eversole said, "Let's plan a vacation together." That went into my heart like an arrow, and I was set on doing it.

In 2006, I traded a week of our Florida timeshare for a place in Branson and invited all the girls. We only had four that year; it was too short notice for 'The Brendas' (Wilson-Fisher and Weeks-Eversole). That was the year we saw the Heaven presentation, thanks to Joanne, who got us the tickets. The time we had together in Branson was off the charts! We got to see The Righteous Brothers and Bill Medley, the only remaining original brother. It brought back so many fun memories from the 1960's. (Bobby Hatfield, the 'brother' that passed away, had a son who sang, and he sounded so authentic.) I also met one of the Gatlin brothers and got his autograph.

We ate and laughed and had a blast and we've gotten together every year since then. We've been to Jacksonville on the beach, Nashville, Indiana in the woods, Arkansas on a beautiful lake, Folly Beach, South Carolina, and Madison, Indiana, where there's a bed and breakfast which suits us fine. In Madison, we love the view of the Ohio River we get to enjoy while we're all sitting on the porch, laughing and chatting away. One year, we got to go on a river cruise down the Ohio.

I can't explain the connection we have, but it's unique and special to all of us. We pray for each other; we've walked through some tough times together. Brenda Eversole lost her husband to cancer. She's an award-winning real estate broker. Penny is a physical therapist. Penny and I met each other when we were three years old and our mothers were in the local

Home Economics Club together and we've been friends ever since (she's my longest standing friend). Her daughter, Courtney, has had two sets of twins! Anne, another friend, is a nurse and has helped me with advice on Cody. Brenda Fisher is a blessing to us, and the life of the party! She plays old songs for us on the piano, and hymns for me, and we're all entertained and blessed. Joanne survived breast cancer and comes to CCM's Indiana Meetings.

I'm a preacher anywhere I go, but they don't pull on me or expect me to be perfect. They accept me – we accept each other – and we pray for each other when we need it. I know it's unusual for us to be this close after all these years, but we are, and we treasure each hour together. It's medicine to my flesh and my soul.

Clifton likes my girlfriends, and he supports my desire to be with them. Our husbands are the best, the way they encourage us to have fun! And the truth is we're better wives and moms when we're happy and free to enjoy our lives.

Chapter 26

Final Thoughts

I close this book with great hope of roses blooming again in all the areas where they're needed. The year 2015 has been a year of restoration for me. Fifteen is three fives. Grace times three! Fifteen – it's also seven (perfection, completion) plus eight (new beginnings). I believe that means there have been some things that needed to be completed, and that I was given a new beginning in completing some unfinished projects (for example, this book) and fulfilling purposes.

I pray that you have been given hope through what I've shared. Life is a tapestry of love and hate, trial and triumph, light and dark. Most of the time, life gives us what we put into it. Life is a field. We sow, and then we reap what we sow. If we keep our eyes on Jesus, and continually renew our minds with the Word of God, the Lord will saturate us with His presence. God sowed Jesus. He is called a Seed (see Galatians 3:16).

As an update on Kelly and our progress in accepting his death, I can truthfully say we do well most of the time. It will be six years this coming October 16th since he went to Heaven. We miss him and we think of him every day. Other people have moved on, and they don't realize the grief over the death of a child is a daily, continual process to work through. When he first passed, my thoughts were, "Why are people laughing? Why are people acting like everything is normal?" The pain was indescribable.

Roses Are Blooming

Something God did for all of us was to connect Darlene with a 'Prince Charming.' After Kelly's passing, she had sunken into the depths of despair and hopelessness. She was as low as she could be. Then, one day in 2012, she received a word from the Lord at one of my Spring Conferences. Glenda Dowd-Tait was teaching with me. Glenda had never met Darlene, but Glenda called her up to the front of the meeting and began to prophesy over her. The prophetic word was that God was preparing a husband for Darlene and that she had given up, but God had a plan. Her new husband would treat her like a queen. She wouldn't have to work because he would take care of her and he would be a threefold cord (see Ecclesiastes 4:12) with Clifton and me.

Darlene hadn't been happy for many years, but when her gentleman showed up two and a half years later, he was all the Lord had said he would be. They were engaged and married and now live in Florida on the ocean. Darlene told me when she got married this time, it was the happiest she'd ever been in her life. A whole new rose bush! Her husband worked in ministry with Clifton back in Colorado and accompanied him to India in 1996.

My daughter, Kami, also has found love and happiness. Roses are blooming all over the place! She is married to someone who loves her, her kids, and God. They purchased a large home on nineteen acres and will be moving in this summer just four miles from town. Their place borders a river. Kami is also stepping up to the plate and using her gifts of teaching and compassion for the elderly. She is seeking to minister in hospice. Good things are ahead and roses are blooming for Kami.

Cody says God speaks to him all the time, and that he's been given a simple revelation on grace to teach to young people and the generation to come. He says he is "on fire" in rehab and dreams of preaching. He thinks about God and his ministry constantly. We were able to visit him recently, and he is different. Cody is coming into the call of God upon his life.

Your children will also be what God has called them to be. As a mother, your part is to pray for them. God has people everywhere, placed strategically, to speak to your child. God loves your child more than you do. He desires for them to prosper and be in health. Have faith! Cody's story is a miracle. You will have one too.

Our middle son, Dustin Frederick, also has a call on his life. He is handsome, funny, a good dad and a joy to have as a son. One high school year he wanted to quit football and just have Bible studies. He knows the power of prayer and the name of Jesus. One night, when he was just seven, he was baptized in the Holy Spirit. Dustin once said he "was called to be either a preacher or a clown." Clifton told him, "Well, if you have a tent, try one and if that fails, you'll already have the tent, so just go with the other." My husband!

Moving Forward

I have forgiven, and hold no bitterness towards anyone for the negative things that happened to me and my family. Writing it all down has brought much healing and restoration, even if the ones causing the pain never said they were sorry or recognized their part in the situations. My point has been that God is faithful and people are just people, at their very best. Human emotions and reactions are not so great when not led and guided by the Holy Spirit. I had my own blame in each circumstance. My saying for life is: "Jesus is Lord, and God is on the throne."

No one knows what the future holds, but when we trust the God of our Salvation, we know who holds every single day of our future. And we know we ultimately hold Heaven in our hearts.

Roses bloom and wilt. Sometimes they are crushed by others. But no matter what happens, we have the promise that, even in the desert, it shall *"Rejoice and blossom as the rose; it shall blossom abundantly and rejoice, even with joy and singing."* (Isaiah 35:1-2)

Be encouraged by my story. No matter what happens, just hang onto our loving God. Your Rose Will Bloom Again!

God Bless You.

Appendix

Recommended Reading on Heaven

"My Dream of Heaven" by Rebecca Ruter Springer (my personal favorite)

"90 minutes in Heaven" by Don Piper (I recommend only the first three chapters)

"The Shack" by William P Young

"Heaven is for Real" by Todd and Colton Burpo

"Confessions of a Grieving Christian" by Zig Ziglar

Kat Kerr has some material on Heaven, and she claims to have been there many times. Someone gave me some CDs of her teachings, and one thing she said that ministered to me was that she'd witnessed a "Cowboy Heaven." I believe it!

How to Be Born Again

As you've read in Chapter 1, my husband and I were born again in a little Baptist church in June, 1970. Our lives were changed forever. Choosing to receive Jesus Christ as your Lord and Savior is the most important decision you'll ever make in your whole life.

Some folks think the term 'born again' means you stop sinning and start attending church, you become religious, or you join a certain group or political persuasion. None of those ideas are correct!

Being born again is how God changes us into His own children. The change on the inside of us (being born again) and the forgiveness of sins that comes along with that change are free gifts that God gives us through Jesus. On the cross, Jesus suffered, died and rose again so you could be born again and become God's precious child. All for free.

How do we receive the free gift? We simply believe good news! God's Word promises, *If you shall confess with your mouth the Lord Jesus, and shall believe in your heart that God has raised Jesus from the dead, you shall be saved... For whosoever shall call upon the name of the Lord shall be saved.* (Romans 10:9, 13, KJV)

God has already done everything to provide salvation. Your part is simply to believe and receive what Jesus has done for you.

If you haven't been born again yet, Jesus is literally standing at the door of your heart right now, and He is knocking, asking to come in to your heart.

You can pray out loud: "Jesus, I confess that You are my Lord and Savior. I believe in my heart that God raised You from the dead. Come into my heart. I open the door of my life to you. Thank You for saving me!"

The very moment you commit your life to Jesus, you're born again. There's a brand-new you! God will always love you and you will *always* be His child.

Please contact me and let us know that you've prayed to receive Jesus as your Savior! I want to help you grow in your new relationship with Jesus. You can contact me through our websites:

www.cliftoncoulterministries.com
www.gracefamilyoutreachchurch.com

I have some free teachings on our websites available under the 'Messages' or 'Teaching/Resources' tabs.

Blessings and Welcome to the Family!

How to Receive the Baptism of the Holy Spirit

By now, you've read my story and you know that I received the baptism of the Holy Spirit in 1977 (see Chapter 2). What a marvelous day! Let me quote a little bit of what happened, "First of all, I was instantly delivered from nicotine. Then, I felt something I'd never experienced before – it was like a flood of pure love pouring over me that I never knew existed. I don't know how long I was on the floor, but I got up from there a different person!"

Jesus promised us that we would receive His power and ability when we are baptized with the Holy Ghost. Jesus said in Acts 1:8, *You shall receive power after the Holy Ghost is come upon you.* God doesn't want you trying to live the 'Christian Life' with your ability. We need His supernatural ability, which comes through the Holy Spirit.

Jesus said that the Holy Spirit is a gift to be received, just by asking. *For every one that asks will receive; and he that seeks will find... And if you know how to give good gifts unto your children: how much more shall your heavenly Father give the Holy Spirit to them that ask him?* (Luke 11:10, 13, KJV)

All you have to do is ask, believe God heard you, and then receive the gift!

Pray: "Father, I need for Your power in my life. Please fill me with the Holy Spirit. Holy Spirit, by faith, I receive You right now! Thank You for baptizing me."

Congratulations! You've been filled with God's supernatural power. There is a supernatural language that comes with the baptism of the Holy Spirit. It's called 'speaking in tongues.' When you prayed, some syllables from a language you don't recognize may rise up from your heart to your mouth (see 1 Corinthians 14:14). Speak them out loud by faith! That is your new prayer language. What you're doing is releasing God's power from the inside by the power of the Holy Spirit. Do this whenever and wherever you like.

It doesn't matter whether you felt anything or not when you prayed to receive the Lord and His Spirit. We receive things from God by faith, not feelings. Jesus explained faith this way: *I say unto you, whatever things you desire, when ye pray,* **believe that ye receive them,** *and (then) you shall have them."* (Mark 11:24, KJV, emphasis mine) Faith believes we receive the answer right when we pray, whether we feel or see anything or not; and then the answer comes.

Please contact me and let me know that you've prayed to be filled with the Holy Spirit. I'd like to rejoice with you and help you grow in your faith. You can contact me through our websites:

www.cliftoncoulterministries.com
www.gracefamilyoutreachchurch.com

I have some free teachings available under the 'Messages' or 'Teaching/Resources' tabs on our websites.

Blessings! You are Loved Forever!

Clifton Coulter Ministries (CCM)

Clifton Coulter Ministries (CCM) is an evangelistic ministry dedicated to soul winning and preaching the gospel of grace and peace. CCM hosts meetings and ladies conferences in the USA and around the world preaching the good news of the unconditional love of God. CCM offers CD teaching series, Christian music and a soul-winning movie, "How the West Was Won," through their website cliftoncoulterministries.com.

After their dramatic conversion to Christ in 1970, Clifton and Geri Coulter immediately began to proclaim the gospel to anyone who would listen. After hosting home group Bible studies, they opened their first church in August of 1977. Clifton and Geri taught at Andrew Wommack's Colorado Bible College (now Charis Bible College) in the 1990s.

Clifton Coulter Ministries celebrated 38 years of evangelistic ministry in August 2015. Miracles and healings regularly accompany their anointed ministry and Clifton and Geri share the Word of God in a humorous and practical way.

Clifton and Geri also pastor Grace Family Outreach Church, located in Park Hills, Missouri. The church website is gracefamilyoutreachchurch.com.

About the Author

Geri Coulter is a pastor's wife, author, popular and dynamic Bible teacher, women's conference speaker, and the host of the weekly radio broadcast, "Oasis of Love." Geri's honest and down-to-earth ministry style is a powerful antidote to the poison of legalistic, lifeless religion.

Geri has been married to Clifton for 47 years. They currently reside in Farmington, Missouri and have four children and twelve grandchildren. As co-founders of Clifton Coulter Ministries, they are enthusiastic ministers of the Gospel of Grace and love to win souls and build up people.

Geri is currently working on her next book, "Nuggets from the Gold Mine," and is looking forward to her first trip to Israel in 2016.

Made in the USA
Monee, IL
10 October 2020

44629815R00148